I0815155

MARKING TIME
with Fabric and Thread

CALENDARS, DIARIES, AND JOURNALS WITHIN YOUR FIBER CRAFT

Tommye McClure Scanlin
Foreword by Sarah C. Swett

Other Schiffer Craft Books by the Author:
Tapestry Design Basics and Beyond: Planning and Weaving with Confidence, foreword by Rebecca Mezoff, ISBN 978-0-7643-6156-2

Other Schiffer Craft Books on Related Subjects:
Threads of Treasure: How to Make, Mend, and Find Meaning through Thread, Sara Barnes, ISBN 978-0-7643-6761-8
Creative Flow: 40 Prescriptions for Tapping Your Creative Impulses, Roberta Bergmann, ISBN 978-0-7643-6308-5
The Art of Weaving a Life: A Framework to Expand and Strengthen Your Personal Vision, Susan Barrett Merrill, instructions by Janet Lewis Estell & Richard Merrill, ISBN 978-0-7643-5264-5

Library of Congress Control Number: 2024932135

All photographs by the author unless otherwise noted in the captions.
Artworks are shown by permission of the artists and photographers noted.

Photograph of *Sonnet without Words* by Archie Brennan is used by permission of Christine Elizabeth Humphrys.

"How to Sing" and excerpt from "GPS" from *With Access to Tools* by Dana Wildsmith, 2023. Reprinted by permission from Madville Publishing, Lake Dallas, Texas.

Interior designed by Llara Pazdan
Type set in Citrus Gothic Solid, Helvetica, and Minion Pro

Front jacket images: Details from artworks by
(*top row, L to R*) Heidi Parkes; Karin Schaller; Natasha Khiev.
(*2nd row, L to R*) Susan Martin Maffei; Karen Turner; Rebecca Cartwright.
(*3rd row, L to R*) Ellen Schiffman; Tommye McClure Scanlin; Linda Watson; Susan Martin Maffei.
(*bottom row, L to R*) Carol Ward; Rowan Haug; Natasha Khiev; Tommye McClure Scanlin.
Front jacket flap: Detail, *Not to Know but to Go On* by Judith Martin.

ISBN: 978-0-7643-6821-9
978-1-5073-0418-1 (Epub)
Printed in China
5 4 3 2

Published by Schiffer Craft
An imprint of Schiffer Publishing, Ltd.
4880 Lower Valley Road
Atglen, PA 19310
Phone: (610) 593-1777; Fax: (610) 593-2002
Email: Info@schifferbooks.com
Web: www.schifferbooks.com

For my husband, Thomas,
who is always encouraging and supportive
and for my sister, Debbie,
who is always steadfast and courageous.

HOW TO SING

To praise my tools, I wear them out. My hoe's
blunt tip is history in 2/2 time,
a simple chopping meter down the rows
of years that rose and fell like breathing. I'm
not finished yet. Whoever is? The work
that weeded me still needs me keeping watch
for what should grow and what should not. The dark,
the daze, the drench, the drought. I doubt I've brought
to fruit two-thirds of what I've planted—dreams,
a child, two dogs for every decade—roots
at last on this old farm I seed and weed
each spring as if it mattered. I love my tools
like friends deep-rooted through our history,
rounding out another year with me.

Dana Wildsmith

With Access to Tools[1]

CONTENTS

See the reverse side of the book jacket for an inspirational guide to Daily Creative Practice Starting Points.

FOREWORD

Holding Time

SARAH C. SWETT

Once upon a time there is a day—an ordinary day to be sure (for that is the best kind), and on this day, somewhere, a stitch is made, a loom is warped, a shape is built, another is completed.

Here the temperature goes up. Over there it rains. Somewhere else, breakfast is delicious. In fact it is exactly like yesterday's breakfast, only not—because the part of the cloth devoted to breakfasts is different than it was a few moments ago: there is new stitch in the cloth, an interesting stripe in the knitting, a bobbin in a fresh color dangling from the fell. Each in its own way says, "This is now."

And that is the point.

For with this needle, that yarn, those bobbins, these hands, someone is marking time in cloth even as it unfolds: the moment, the weeks, the years, the decades becoming fabric a day at a time.

It is how we remember. It is how we know we are here. It is why Tommye wrote this wonderful book.

For in these pages, writer, teacher, weaver, and devoted diarist Tommye Scanlin celebrates the practice of marking time with textiles. Mingling her personal evolution as a weaver of tapestry diaries with the wisdom of other textile timekeepers, she interlaces pleasure and possibility with theory and practice. Here she has created a book inspiring enough that if I weren't already doing this, I'd start immediately.

And actually I still can. I've been a diarist for decades, so unexpected ideas have always been at the heart of my practice, and who can resist exploring? Weaving moments into massive tapestries, drawing daily comics of looms and cloth, knitting everyday sweaters from the fleeces of sheep whose names I know—each is a way to hold on to time. In my most recent tapestries the weft of used coffee filters indicates how long it took to generate my materials: one dark/light stripe per filter, one filter (and two tiny cups of coffee), per day. And while the designs do not shout "diary," each nevertheless marks time in its own way. So you see, I never know what is going to show up next.

I cannot now remember why I began this work, but I know I continue for the thrill of it. Anticipation, adrenaline, satisfaction—that frisson of delight that shows up again and again when hands, yarn, pencils, and imagination come together—I can't do without the daily micro-drama. Like breakfast, each iteration is both brand new and utterly familiar. It is exciting and soothing at once and, for me, downright addictive.

Also, whatever else happens, I get to impress myself just a tiny bit, over and over. "Yay me!"

What joy, then, that Tommye has gathered all these devoted textile-centric timekeepers into a book.

The camaraderie alone would be wondrous, but because everyone shares the whys and wherefores of their practice and point of view, we readers are freed from any notion that there is only one way to do this. Indeed, the breadth of work leaves me breathless even as the suggestions for jumping-off points make my hands itch to experiment: colors, numbers, dreams, dance, dice, knotting, netting . . . so much possibility for fresh work. And always the understanding that once begun, the work will evolve and unfold as we explore.

Marking time in cloth is a practice of centuries and brand new every day, and I am so grateful that Tommye has brought it to the fore in these pages. Together and alone, she invites each of us to record our individual experiences in ways that are compelling enough to begin, intriguing enough to continue, and pleasurable enough to be anticipated with glee.

All we need to do, each time, is pick up our tools and start.

Yay us!

Once upon a time, there is a day . . .

Author and artist Sarah C. Swett shares stories from her life experiences through her tapestries, in her writings, and on social media. @sarahcswett

Sarah C. Swett, *Time*, 2023. Handwoven tapestry: 3" × 5". Weft: linen, wool, natural dyes; warp: silk. Photo: Sarah C. Swett.

1

BEGINNINGS: FINDING A CREATIVE PATH

CHAPTER 1

> Be bold, sang Time. This year,
> Be bold, sang Time,
> For when you honor yesterday,
> Tomorrow ye will find.[2]
>
> —AMANDA GORMAN

Have you ever had an idea that just kept bugging you? One that would fade away for a while but then return to say: "What would happen if . . . ?" Maybe one day you decided to see what *would* happen if you listened to your idea. In my case, paying attention to one of these ideas started me on a journey that I am still traveling.

Tommye Scanlin, working on the 2017 tapestry diary on a galvanized pipe loom. Photo: Thomas E. Scanlin.

The journey involves my art practice. I am a tapestry weaver. Like all weaving, handwoven tapestries have two basic components: warp and weft. The warp threads are put onto a loom, stretched under tension. The warp is almost like a skeleton for the weaving, since the weft yarns cover and hide those threads as they are woven. Weft yarns usually do not travel from edge to edge of the warp, being woven only in the places a certain color is needed in the design. The weaver manipulates many wefts across each row. This is one of the reasons tapestry weaving is a slow process.

For me, part of the appeal of tapestry weaving *is* the slowness of the process. Thread by thread, the tapestry grows on the loom as I weave. Days, weeks, or months are spent on each piece, depending on how large or complex it is. I devote many hours sitting at the loom, placing the wefts into the warp threads and making decisions as I weave. There's time to think about what has been woven and what is still to come. The empty warp is steadily filled with weft as something much more than the individual threads is created.

Gradually I began to relate the tapestries I was weaving to the passing of time. I began to wonder if the tapestry process itself could be used to represent time. What if I made a tapestry with each day as a separate, distinct part? I could weave a little bit daily. On each new day I could look back at what was done before and add to that. The empty warp threads would be ahead, waiting to be filled with the wefts I would select as the days arrived. The tapestry would become a tangible record of my experience of time as it passed.

I knew that other visual artists had daily practices in their chosen fields, like photography or painting.[3] Many people faithfully keep daily sketchbooks and journals. At first I thought that my medium of tapestry, indeed any textile medium, did not lend itself readily to a daily practice because it is slower than sketching or photographing. The small steps used in a textile technique are somewhat meaningless until the larger piece is completed. Even so, for one month in May 2008, I decided to see where a daily tapestry practice would lead. Later I will describe more about my adventure with this idea, which I call my tapestry diaries.

Over the next few years, I wrote about my daily tapestry practice both in print and on social media and used the idea as the topic for a couple of workshops. Other tapestry weavers started their versions of tapestry diaries and described them on their blogs and other social media. It was exciting to see more and more tapestry artists embracing the idea of tapestry diaries and creating their own versions. In fact, in 2017 I curated an exhibit of the work of six individuals who were doing tapestry diaries: *Time Warp—and Weft* at the Lyndon House Art Center, Athens, Georgia. Featured were weavings by Janet Austin, Geri Forkner, Janette Meetze, Rebecca Mezoff, Kathy Spoering, and myself.

I continued to be intrigued about the concept of daily practice; I knew there must be those who used different fiber and fabric mediums in this approach. I began to ask people who worked in other mediums if they had a daily practice or could direct me to others who did. I found that there are indeed many who are creating or adapting their fiber or fabric mediums as calendars, diaries, or journals. For instance, Kay Lawrence, whom I heard about through a friend, had done a tapestry in which she daily recorded her emotional state during a yearlong relationship breakup in 1981. Instagram soon led me to others, including Natasha Khiev, who was creating a small tapestry each day and posting the result on her Instagram account.[4]

Kay Lawrence, *Diary* (detail of the beginning months), 1981. Handwoven tapestry: 13 × 98 cm (5" × 38.5"), 8 warps per inch. Cotton warp; wool, cotton, linen weft. Photo: Kay Lawrence.

Natasha Khiev, 100 images from January 2023–April 2023, 2.5" to 4.5" square. Photo courtesy of Natasha Khiev.

As I explored the concept of recording time with textiles, I found the work of those using climate data to create works that record weather conditions and temperature ranges over spans of time. Data visualization in the form of textiles can be experienced in a more tactile and visceral way than charts and graphs seen in publications or in a digital presentation. In a Zoom chat with Asy Connelly and Emily McNeil, two of the founders of the Tempestry Project, I learned of Jordan Cunliffe's book *Record, Map & Capture in Textile Art*, in which are found many examples of data visualization in cloth and stitch.

Joan Sheldon, *Sky Scarf*, 2015. Crocheted: 75" × 6" Tunisian crochet stitch pattern. Alpaca. Sheldon's *Sky Scarf* was inspired by Lea Redmond's version in the book *Knit the Sky*. Courtesy of Joan Sheldon, photos credit: Wade Sheldon Photography.

Rebecca Cartwright, *Temperature Quilt* (detail), 2019. Quilt: 66" × 77". Cotton, hand- and machine-appliquéd split hexagons depicting high temperature above low temperature. Photo: Rebecca Cartwright.

Cunliffe's book led me also to consider how codes are used to transmit or even hide ideas or information. Although the idea of codes doesn't at first glance seem to relate to the daily practice concept I'd begun writing about, I realized that there were examples of coded information contained in some of my own tapestry diaries, as well as in the work of some of the others who were included in the book. For instance, one of the tapestries by Kay Lawrence in which she converted the alphabet into different values of gray to transcribe a poem, and ones by Susan Martin Maffei in which she encoded significant dates by using knotted cords or quipus. In my case, one example was my use of a version of a shield knot symbol I wove into the tapestries made during the years my nephew was deployed on active military duty in the Middle East.

Susan Martin Maffei, *Nessa Nessa Winter Moon*, 2014. Handwoven tapestry and mixed media: 252" full length; 20" × 9" × 8" when closed. Tapestry is hand-spun wool warp, indigo-dyed silks, Bulgarian silks, wool, linen, hemp, cotton, and metallic wefts. Mount is acid-free book board, fabric, acid-free Canson paper and glues. The tapestry is mounted on a series of 28 screens arranged as an accordion book. It can be viewed in many ways—circular, accordion, or stretched out to its full length. When closed it is a compact large book.

Calendars, diaries, journals, data visualization, symbols, and codes used by those designing with fibers—I found connecting threads leading around the world as I began to unravel the concept of recording the passing of time with textile techniques! I reached out to many individuals, asking if they would be willing to share images of and details about their practice for this book. To those individuals, I asked these three questions:

- What is (or was) your journaling or daily practice?
- Why are you doing it—what was the initial motivation and why do you sustain the practice?
- How do you do it—what's the medium, the process, the end product?

Tommye Scanlin, *Tapestry Diary* (detail), 2008. This shows a shield knot symbol at the top. Photo: Tommye Scanlin.

I hope you'll be as inspired as I have been by the creations of the artists whose work is included here. Maybe, encouraged by what their practice means to them, you'll be moved to begin the process of recording the passing of time in your own way.

Let's begin with words from Linda Watson, who describes how her daily practice of what she calls Listening guides her days and is an invitation for what's to come.

Ayesha Barlas, *100 Days Project Scotland* tapestries, exhibited in *Tapestry 5: Time and Place*, Patriothall Gallery, Edinburgh, Scotland, November 2022. Photo courtesy of Ayesha Barlas.

Carol Ward, journal with watercolors and small loom, ready to weave. Courtesy of Carol Ward.

Karen Turner, *Stitch Journal* (detail), 2022. Stitched: approximately 1-inch area. Vintage French metis (blend of cotton and linen) bedsheet, hand-dyed silk, and cotton thread. Photo courtesy of Karen Turner.

Judith Martin, *Not to Know but to Go On*, 2010–2013. Mixed-media fabric: 66.75 meters h × 35.5 cm w × 1 cm d (73 yards × 14" × 0.4"). Artist canvas, found fabrics, cotton embroidery floss, cotton tape; couching of found fabrics done by hand. Shown installed in World of Threads Festival, 2014, in Oakville, Ontario. Photo: Frank Meyers.

Listening

LINDA WATSON

WESTMINSTER, CALIFORNIA

> Warping a loom and Listening are more of a beckoning, a beginning, a possibility, an invitation. They are ways to get ready for what is yet to come, the actions that will need to be taken, and an act of trust that something *is* coming.

Linda Watson began weaving warp-faced and brocade landscapes more than 40 years ago. Now she is following an ongoing internal nudge to learn tapestry. Her current tapestry work revolves around a project titled "Stories My Mother Told Me" and involves a garden, a mural, sacred texts, and reliquaries.

My daily practice is one of Listening. Listening is similar to mindfulness or contemplative prayer, but without a tradition or any rules, guidelines, or suggestions. Also, unlike mindfulness or contemplative prayer, Listening is a call to action, albeit usually a small action. It tends to answer the question "What next?" For me, it happens throughout the day but is particularly prominent in the morning. Sometimes, just waking up, I hear, or see, a part of a weaving I'm working on, or maybe a sentence or two, or perhaps a song. I know that is what and where I need to focus that day.

Some people call this intuition, and I think that's at least partially true. But I find that intuition is a bit more nebulous. Listening is physically present; it arrives through one of my senses: hearing, seeing, feeling, smelling, or taste. Sometimes I hear a bit of a song, someone's conversation, or, seemingly out of nowhere, a voice. Being a very visual person, I'm more apt to see an image, softly blurred, or notice something in real life, a chair, and a color. I may feel a nudge, gentle but insistent, yes, that way or no, not that way, or just a feeling of knowing that somehow that's the way or the right thing to do.

In that way, as a tool, Listening is a lot like the warp on a loom. While a warp requires a decision as to sett, size, and fiber, a decision can also be made to Listen. But warp alone does not a weaving make. Nor does Listening alone make a practice that can help me and benefit my life. Warping a loom and Listening are more of a beckoning, a beginning, a possibility, an invitation. They are ways to get ready for what is yet to come, the actions that will need to be taken, and an act of trust that something *is* coming. That same loom warped eight different times, with the same sett and materials, can hold eight different images—sunsets, flowers, a cat, a child's portrait, color samples—many, many possibilities, all beginning with that warp. Listening is like that warp in that the action to be taken may show up differently, but it is the act of Listening that sets up the space for it to happen, for one thing to flow into another.

Linda Watson, *Changing Path*. This is a view of a trail within the gardens at Rancho Los Alamitos in Long Beach, California, only a few miles from her home. Linda walks here often while practicing Listening. Photo courtesy of Linda Watson.

Linda Watson, *Sunflower*, 2018. Handwoven tapestry: 12.5" × 14". This is the first image of 12. There will be four panels, three images on each, progressing through the color wheel. Photo courtesy of Linda Watson.

The image shows some of the result of my practice of Listening, planned as a four-panel piece. The first panel of the four is complete, with the yellow sunflower at the bottom. Above it will be yellow-green feverfew leaves in the middle, and then large green anthurium leaves at the top. Next panel will have blue-green, blue, and blue-violet and so on into the next two panels, working around the color wheel. Each of the flowers I'm depicting is from my yard and approximately the same size, with the gradating triangles between them and as borders. It's quite a juggle finding the right color of flower and then making it all work together in terms of size and shape.

I started the project in 2018 as a new tapestry weaver in order to learn to weave tapestry, after 40+ years of weaving wall hangings on a floor loom, using warp-faced weaves, brocade, and painted warps. I knew this color wheel / flower project was way beyond my tapestry ability, but had no idea just how much. Consequently it took me four years to weave the first panel! Yes, there were a few other projects along the way, but still . . . And I learned. I learned about cartoons, simplifying, using Photoshop to help design along with my watercolors, and maybe most importantly, is it weaveable? I had to listen very closely for what was next since I was so often out of my weaving comfort zone. I also wanted to shake up my color usage and understanding of acid dyes, and that is definitely happening as I am foregoing my usual "a little of this and a little of that" painterly approach to dyes, and am taking the time to measure, record, and compare. ”

Heidi Parkes, *Meuse, Pandemic, Invisible, Sweetheart*, 2020. Quilt: 60" × 60". Mostly cotton fabric and thread; hand pieced, hand embroidered, and hand quilted. Photo credit: Daniel McCollough.

This diaristic quilt tracked the pandemic for 100 days, beginning on April 7, 2020. "This daily (sometimes weekly . . .) practice of adding to the quilt top helped me to track the days, and to remember that time was passing during a historical moment."

2

OBSERVATIONS OF TIME IN TEXTILES: CALENDARS, DIARIES, AND JOURNALS

CHAPTER 2

> Like sands through the hourglass, so are the days of our lives.[5]

Many of us have kept a diary or journal. Maybe you started a diary when you were young and for a while told "Dear Diary" what was happening in your life. Later a journal may have been a place to make notes about things to remember or insights that occurred to you. Maybe you wrote in your journal occasionally and not daily. As for calendars, we track our plans with digital versions or even the "old school" paper day planners and wall calendars.

Tommye Scanlin, a selection of journals. Photo: Chris Dant.

I have used all of those methods at one time or another. When I was 10 or 11 years old, I was given a little white-leather book that had a lock and a tiny key. "My Diary" was stamped in gold on the front. I wrote in it faithfully every day at first but lost interest after a few months. I wonder what happened to that little diary? It was packed away with other childhood things, I guess, all now long gone.

Looking back to the timekeeping methods you used earlier in your life and also how you do it now could be great starting places as you consider beginning to celebrate the passing of time with your fiber works. Journaling is a practice I have maintained off and on for many years. In my journal I write about both the designing and weaving process of my tapestries. I spill out my perceived inadequacies with art making but also celebrate accomplishments in the pages. I revisit the journal pages from time to time to see what I was thinking earlier or to check details about works in progress.

Since 2009 I have been a faithful writer of "morning pages" as described by Julia Cameron in *The Artist's Way*.[6] Her book offers suggestions of activities to help break through creative impasses. One of those is the writing of morning pages. This is a practice in which you write three pages by hand in a stream-of-consciousness way, not editing, censoring, or ever rereading what you have written.

Doing the morning pages has become an important part of my daily routine. I arise early and write for about 30 or 45 minutes. I have found this is a good way to ease into the day. These few minutes of writing allow me to have a bit of time to reflect about what I have accomplished, everything from getting the laundry done to thinking about an upcoming exhibit of my tapestries. Worries can be written down as well as hopes and dreams for myself, for family members, and for the state of the world. Even though I don't reread the daily entries, giving myself the time to "voice" my feelings by writing them out helps my emotional well-being.

Rowan Haug working on *All My Quiet Moments*, 2020. Photo courtesy of Rowan Haug.

Even if you don't maintain an ongoing diary or journal, most likely you are still acutely aware of the passing of time. Alarm clocks or phone alerts tell you when to rise. A timer lets you know that the clothes dryer has stopped, or the roast should come out of the oven. How often do you use the alert on your mobile phone as a reminder about an upcoming event a week, a day, or even an hour before it happens?

I keep track of my schedule digitally these days, but I do miss the spiral-bound monthly planners I used for many years. They had only small squares allotted for each day, but I can still flip back through old ones to see what I was doing on any particular day. As I think about it now, those monthly planner calendars were really stand-ins for diary keeping.

All these things—diaries, journals, and calendars—have a direct relationship to the way we experience and understand our time. Think about the many ways we talk about time, either directly or indirectly. "If I only had time enough, I would (fill in the blank with your own wish)." The Rolling Stones told us that time is on our side. Yes, it is. Want to find other timeworn phrases? Put "time quotes" into the search bar and you'll be amazed at how many turn up. A few years ago, I was astonished when I heard a podcast speaker mention that the very word "time" is the most frequently used noun in the English language, according to the Oxford English Corpus.[7] An online search took me to the Oxford English Dictionary site, where I found confirmation of that, as well as that the words "year" and "day" are also among the most commonly used, with "year" at number three and "day" at number five in frequency of use.

It seems we humans have been attentive to time and found ways to keep track of it throughout history. Early measurements of time were based on familiar experiences of daylight and night, the phases of the moon, and the seasons. Instruments to mark and record time were made in Babylonia and Egypt at least 5,000 years ago.[8]

Making note of what happened over time also began thousands of years ago. The earliest known diary example might be several papyrus logbooks dealing with the transportation of limestone to Giza for use in the Great Pyramid. Known collectively as *The Book of Merer*, they were written over 4,500 years ago.[9]

In 14th-century China, a famous calligrapher and painter of the Yuan dynasty, Bi Guo, wrote what is known as the *Yunshan Diary*. In it he often described daily weather conditions. Twenty-first-century scientists have used his diary entries from September 1308 to December 1309 in their studies of climate change.[10]

There are many other well-known historical examples of diaries, like those of Samuel Pepys. Pepys wrote over a million words in his six volumes of diaries between 1660 and 1669. Pepys's accounts of his life and times documented not only daily trivia, like what he had for meals, but also major events like the Great Plague (1665–1666) and the Great Fire of London (1666).[11] One of the most touching records of a life is *The Diary of a Young Girl* by Anne Frank, written as she and her family were in hiding from Nazis during World War II.

In the latter part of the 20th century, diary and journal writing began to be recommended for therapeutic benefits as well as for documenting one's life events. In the 1960s and 1970s, Dr. Ira Progoff developed what came to be known as the Intensive Journal method. He conducted Intensive Journal workshops throughout the United States and Canada in which participants were guided to use writing exercises as a way to gain insight into different aspects of their lives.[12]

Now we have ways to record every second of our lives—and to share those moments through social media, if we want. But our 21st-century interest in recording time and its passing is not unique. After all, we humans have done it for centuries. Animals? According to science, each species understands time in its own way, following genetic cues, instinct, and the cycles of nature.[13]

My own daily tapestry practice has been engaging to me for years. Gradually, I became curious about others who might be responding to the passage of time with their own textile mediums. Through research done in libraries, in interviews, and through social media connections, I've found myriad creative ways people document their lives with fiber and fabric. Join me for a fascinating look at a few of the calendars, diaries, and journals that are being stitched, pieced, knitted, and woven every day.

Janet Austin, *2018 Tapestry Diary* (detail). Photo: Janet Austin.

Calendars and Diaries

JANET AUSTIN

EAST GREENWICH, RHODE ISLAND

When people ask, "Do you have a new year's resolution?," I have a simple answer. Yes, I will weave every weekday. I have learned the secret to keeping a resolution: choose one that you actually look forward to; resolve to do something you really want to do, and you will follow through.

Janet Austin fell in love with weaving in 1972 at Massachusetts College of Art, where she imagined herself becoming expert in every fiber technique from basketry to knotless netting. After eight years trying to earn a living from handwoven scarves, shawls, rugs, purses, ponchos, pillows, etc., she felt the urge to create images and earned an MFA in painting at UNC Greensboro. Serendipity brought the weaving and painting together in 1983, and a tapestry weaver was born. Janet weaves, paints, lectures, and teaches in Rhode Island.

" Before I started this daily practice, New Year's Day meant nothing to me. Now it's an exciting time of year, as I cut off one diary and prepare the warp for the next one. By November, I'm bored with the current diary, and wondering what I can do with the next one that will satisfy my thirst for something new and different.

I wove my first tapestry diary in 2010. For years I had thought about doing some kind of weaving that would mark the passing of time. When I was 11, my family moved to Denmark, and my mother took up counted cross-stitch. I still have a lovely book of patterns from that time, featuring a different stylized bird for each month. In 2009, I was following Tommye Scanlin's tapestry blog and was intrigued by her tapestry diary, so I decided to give it a try.

In the very first week of that very first tapestry diary, I learned a lesson. I sat down at the loom and saw what I had woven the previous day. I didn't like it, and for a second I thought I would just unweave it, but then it hit me: today is today, yesterday is done and cannot be changed. I must move on and go forward. This was the first time that I saw the tapestry diary as a metaphor for life. At the end of the year, when I unwound the diary from my loom and cut it off, I was amazed. There it was—a year! Any individual days that weren't perfect did not spoil the effect of the whole. After all, what's one day out of 365?

On January 2, 2010, I attended my mother's memorial service and felt the need to mark that in the diary somehow. Soon I marked my daughter's birthday, the day my cat went blind, and the first US game of the World Cup. It was an eventful year and an eventful tapestry diary. Since that year, I have marked only the occasional exceptional days, because the practice has become more of a tapestry weaving and design exercise and less of a personal diary; but in 2020, it seemed wrong not to acknowledge what was going on. How could I weave while in the days of a pandemic without making some reference to it? As I wove each day, answers came to me.

On a practical note, which loom to use is still an unresolved issue for me. For the first year I used a floor loom but didn't like having it unavailable for other projects. However, I can put a long warp on the floor loom, then cut off and retie each year. And it's also faster weaving with foot treadles. On the other hand, I can't take it with me when I travel like I have with the pipe looms or Mirrix. There's the dilemma of what to do with the times when I'm away, as my husband and I frequently travel. One of my decisions has been to weave an extra day each day before and after my trips. But it's a little unsettling to be weaving days that are in the future . . . !

However, I've found weaving daily has become a habit, just like not weaving daily can be (sadly). During the first year, I didn't realize how much this

Janet Austin. *2016 Tapestry Diary*. Handwoven tapestry: 21" × 8". Cotton warp, mostly wool weft with cotton and silk. Photo: Janet Austin.

practice had become a part of my life until one day when I was moping around, feeling sad. Suddenly I realized, "I haven't woven the diary today!" It cheered me up to have that small thing to look forward to!

Like many artists, sometimes I feel resistance, I procrastinate and avoid the studio. Perhaps that new tapestry is giving me trouble and I'm not sure what to do. Other times, it's going really well and I'm afraid I'll ruin it! The diary is unthreatening, as it involves only a simple decision, and it lures me into the studio. Once I have completed the diary entry, I'm in weaving mode, and I look around to see what else I can do.

In order to have an unthreatening tapestry diary, there must be rules; even so, they're my rules, so I can break them if I want to! The rules provide a framework, so I only have a simple decision to make each day. Which of these three colors will I use today? For my first diary, I wove a parallelogram each day, seven of them across the warp so one line represented one week. I chose a limited color palette each month and changed the direction of the parallelograms each month.

I like to start the year weaving something very simple because that gives me room to grow. Around late April, I start getting bored with the simple rectangle or parallelogram I am weaving every day, but I continue, because I know it's in that boredom that the creative ideas will sneak in. I know something will come to me, usually a small change that still leaves room for the next idea. Maybe I add a stripe. Or I divide my daily shape in two . . . but how to divide it? Horizontally, vertically, or diagonally? By June or July, something different is happening. By October, I'm getting carried away, weaving leaves or clouds. By December, I start looking forward to the next year, when I can start simply once again.

Janet Austin. *2019 Tapestry Diary*. Handwoven tapestry: 24" × 9". Cotton warp, mostly wool, and wool/polyester blend, with cotton. Photo: Janet Austin.

Janet Austin. *2018 Tapestry Diary*. Handwoven tapestry: 21" × 15". Cotton warp, mostly wool weft with linen, silk, rayon, cotton. Photo: Janet Austin.

Janet Austin. *2020 Tapestry Diary*. Handwoven tapestry: 39" × 9.5". Wool warp, mostly wool weft, some cotton and rayon. Photo: Janet Austin.

Now, as a year ends, when people ask, "Do you have a new year's resolution?," I have a simple answer. Yes, I will weave every weekday. I have learned the secret to keeping a resolution: choose one that you actually look forward to. Resolve to do something you really want to do, and you will follow through. ”

AYESHA BARLAS

SPEAR BRIDGE, UNITED KINGDOM

Weaving a new tapestry every day not only facilitated an intense immersion that helped me distill some ideas that had been simmering on the back burner, it was also instructive and thought provoking as I was able to practice, improve, and apply the techniques learned, translating them into my designs daily.

Ayesha Barlas is a textile artist and painter based in the Scottish Highlands. In 2019, her work was shortlisted for the Cordis Showcase in Edinburgh. Since then, she has taken part in the 100 Days Project Scotland. @ayeshabarlas

“A lifelong interest in the creative arts, a passion for making things, and finding myself living in the Scottish Highlands, where a strong weaving tradition persists, all paved a direct path leading me to tapestry weaving. It is a path that I want to tread with care, guided by my love for the craft and the desire to fine-hone my skills while pushing the limits of the medium.

When the pandemic turned the whole world askew, I was at the tail end of a two-year weaving course with Fiona Hutchison, an Edinburgh-based tapestry weaver and educator. To keep the momentum going and my nascent weaving practice alive in the vacuum created by the lockdown, I decided to participate in the 100 Days Project. This is a cross-disciplinary online art project that takes place every spring; it gives participants a chance to choose one creative exercise, repeat it every day for 100 consecutive days, record it, and share it on Instagram; www.100daysscotland.co.uk.

By committing to the 100 Days Project, not only was I able to provide myself a framework within which to explore my creativity, but, more importantly, it became the perfect means to better my daily studio discipline. The requirement to work relatively quickly and to have a finished piece by the end of each day entailed a sense of urgency and pressure to produce work, which was useful. While the complexity of each piece was different, with some feeling more resolved than others, having a finished piece every day was gratifying. It also fostered a playful approach, which has fed back into my practice, making me more adventurous in my experiments with color, texture, and unusual materials to express my thoughts and emotions. Each tapestry I weave is a tangible manifestation of an internal dialogue, representing the interplay between my thoughts and their physical expression, with materiality being as important as the subject matter.

Ayesha Barlas, *Skies*, 2020. Handwoven tapestry: 6 cm × 6 cm (2.36" × 2.36"). Cotton warp, assorted fibers for weft. A series of the daily tapestries as part of the 100 Day Project Scotland, all showing skies of various hues. Photo courtesy of Ayesha Barlas.

Ayesha Barlas, *100 Days Project Scotland*, 2020. Ayesha Barlas standing with installation of her tapestries on exhibit in *Tapestry 5: Time and Place*, Patriothall Gallery in Edinburgh, Scotland, November 2022. Photo courtesy of Ayesha Barlas.

For this project my brief to myself was to weave a 6-by-6-centimeter tapestry doodle a day, which turned out to be wonderfully simple and deceptively challenging. I wanted each piece to be an exercise underpinned by interplay between spontaneity and more considered decision-making. Mobility being a prerequisite to weave a tapestry a day for 100 days, a portable loom meant that I could carry my weaving into the living room, or the garden, or take it along on a hike. I travel a lot between Edinburgh and the Highlands and like to weave on the train, so a small loom was the obvious and practical choice.

I used the same cotton warp for most doodles, though the weft did vary greatly. Giving in to my inner magpie, I have bought and acquired wool, linen, cotton, silk, and metallic thread at every opportunity, so I had an eclectic mix of yarns to experiment with. My project brief was an opportunity to do just that, and some of the yarns actually inspired the design and theme of what I was going to weave. The subtle colorway of my Shetland yarns, reminiscent of the colors of the Highland lochs, led me to explore the patterns created by the play of light on the surface of the dark peaty waters. In contrast, the bright, happy colors of the cotton yarns dictated a series of festive tapestries, including a tiny prayer tapestry comprising 100 rya knots of colored yarn symbolizing 100 prayers for the healing of the world in these dire times. This piece was inspired by the cross-cultural practice of tying bits of textiles to trees as a physical representation of prayer, such as the Clootie trees of Scotland and Ireland and the Shaman trees of central Asia.

To make the project bite-sized, I divided it into themes, starting with the color spectrum. Eventually the theme selection became serendipitous, drawing on various sources, including my existing artworks and objects around the house. For example, the leaf of a calathea plant in the living room made an appearance in one of the doodles. Within each theme there were mini-explorations of various techniques learnt—eccentric weaving to interpret the river, rya knots to depict a cloud, and a ginkgo leaf picked up on a hike that leant itself to a shaped tapestry, to name a few.

While the first pandemic year of 2020 was underwhelming in many ways, the void created by the travel restrictions allowed me to explore more of my beloved Highland landscape. A walk in the local woodland when the bluebells were in full bloom inspired yet another set of doodles. These tapestries explore the transition of the figurative to the abstract and how abstracted shapes and colors can convey a sense of place. Some of the landscape tapestries also explore the moods of the summer skies from dawn to midnight. I love to weave en plein air, and quite a few pieces have been woven outside in the garden, inspired by the views from it.

The project was challenging but rewarding. It made me delve into my creative reserves, develop creative resilience, and expand my tapestry-weaving skills. I was able to carve out a dedicated weaving time, a morning ritual of getting to the loom before the day took over. Weaving a new tapestry every day not only facilitated an intense immersion which helped me distill some ideas that had been simmering on the back burner, it was also instructive and thought provoking as I was able to practice, improve, and apply the techniques learned, translating them into my designs daily.

The daily sharing by all the participants in the 100 Days Project helped build a community that encouraged and motivated each other. I was inspired and in complete awe of so much creative discipline, which helped strengthen my own focus. Though not all days were equal, I tried to make focusing a mindful daily exercise. The aim was not only to experiment and challenge myself to step out of my comfort zone, but also to explore, have fun, and weave a little every day. ”

KATE COLWELL

KENSINGTON, CALIFORNIA

> The longer I weave them, the more I understand that part of me rejoices in the freedom to break rules. Even my own rules.

Kate Colwell has been involved with textiles since 1960 and learned to weave at San Francisco Fiber in 1981. As a part-time floor loom weaver for 35 years, she predominantly wove functional gifts for family and friends, but her work increasingly focused on reuse and recycling as well as repurposing found objects. Over the past 20 years she has added spinning, knitting, dyeing, basket making, and tapestry to her creative work. Many of her tapestries focus on current issues as well as the diaries that reflect emotions, places, and experiences from her travels.

“I began weaving tapestry in November 2016, and during the next months I wove many small tapestries, including a series on trips to Mexico and Guatemala. These reflected specific scenes from the trips rather than a daily practice.

In 2017, I learned of the concept of a daily tapestry diary and decided to create my first diary to mark my birthday month in April. I used a children's lap loom to weave images of each day, including a new car, a wedding, a school reunion, and other occasions. My genre is narrative tiny tapestries, so throughout 2017 I also wove tapestries of outings and events. Then, in 2018, I again resolved to weave daily and to create tapestry diaries for each month.

February 2018 took me back to my beloved Guatemala. The strips for a monthly diary required a long loom, so I decided to weave one small Travel Diary for each week of my three-week journey. Tapestry wool does not exist in Guatemala, so my first decision was to use a wool warp from home and embroidery floss as weft, knowing that I could find

Kate Colwell, *First Diary April 2017*, 2017. Handwoven tapestry: 11.5" × 2.75". Photo by Brittany Bradley, courtesy of Kate Colwell.

a thread store in most towns if I was missing a desired color. These followed a strip linear pattern of a block for each day. In the first two weeks I was working with weavers around Lake Atitlan. Those days were filled with incredible colors and sights, and I started evolving my definition of what my Travel Diaries would be. Each evening I would weave an image, event, or feeling from the day. These were woven while waiting for transportation or sitting in a hotel room or outside watching a sunset.

My little looms have been great conversation starters. I weave in public, and in a country like Guatemala, where most Indigenous people generally have some familiarity with weaving, both local people and tourists stop and talk. One of my biggest surprises was when two young boys, about 10 and 13, came over to where I was weaving in the central plaza in the city of Antigua. I explained what I was doing, and each said that he knew I was weaving, as he was a weaver. It turns out they were Indigenous children who were floor loom weavers from the western provinces but who were out of work; their families sent them to Antigua to work as ambulatory vendors of trinkets in the park. They understood weaving and were interested to learn that I was doing weft-faced images as opposed to their balanced (or warp-faced) weaving.

Kate Colwell, *Travel Diary—Guatemala*, 2019. Handwoven tapestry: 8" × 10" overall, individual weavings 2.25" × 6". Photo by Brittany Bradley, courtesy of Kate Colwell.

Kate Colwell, *One Day at a Time, One Step at a Time*, fall 2020. Handwoven tapestry: 8.25" × 6.25". Photo by Brittany Bradley, courtesy of Kate Colwell.

Through 2018 and into early 2020 I continued to travel domestically and in Guatemala. Each day of a trip I would weave a block of my Travel Diary commemorating a place or emotion or event. So far I have done more than two dozen Travel Diaries that serve as wonderful mementos of my travels.

The pandemic was hard on everyone and as autumn 2020 arrived, I had a dark time, which I marked in tiny rectangles to reflect my emotions each day. I was away from home for two months, but unlike my other Travel Diaries, this was exclusively a record of emotions. The title, *One Day at a Time, One Step at a Time*, was a reminder to myself each day not to take on more than my overwhelmed heart could bear.

My Travel Diaries continue to evolve to meet my current needs. The longer I weave them, the more I understand that part of me rejoices in the freedom to break rules. Even my own rules. At home I still study and do weaving exercises. I create planned weavings with cartoons and carefully chosen colors. It seems that since I have spent so much of my life as a rule follower, I need the spontaneity of a Travel Diary, which lets me break free of all the "shoulds."

But spontaneity comes with a cost. On the road I don't have time to unweave, and I accept my works with their flaws. I eyeball things and then have to live with the results. There is no perspective. Selvedges are wonky. But still, for me, the joy and freedom outweigh those discomforts. ❞

Geri Forkner, *Daily Weaving*, 2005/2006. Weavings: 3" × 3" approximately, joined by stitching. Assorted found papers and other items.

GERI FORKNER

SWEETWATER, TENNESSEE

Now, many years later, what began as a whim has blossomed into a large collection of strips and squares asking for further interpretations. The collection has become a metaphor for everyday life, both its universality and its consequences on the environment. Overall the pieces speak to an "alternate reality" reflective of the many different ways people perceive the same event and how time alters that perception.

Geri Forkner creates felted and woven works of art from her studio in Tennessee. She exhibits and teaches fiber arts internationally to both children and adults and is the recipient of an Appalachian Craft and Culture Fellowship from Arrowmont School of Arts and Crafts. A member of the Southern Highland Craft Guild, Geri cherishes the old traditions and skills while using fibers in innovative ways.

“On January 1, 2005, I started making a 3-inch-square weaving every day using only found items. In the back of my mind, I wanted to see if I could finish out the year. At the end of the year I knew it wasn't finished. I had no overall vision for this project originally other than making one thing every day using something that came into my life that day.

All the weavings are done off loom. The individual pieces are usually zigzag-stitched together in long rows. Some have machine- or hand-stitching embellishments. For example, the 3-inch-square ones are wrapped and needle-woven on mat board. Paper is either cut or torn and rewoven into itself, held in place either with machine stitching when I'm home or staples when I'm away. That usually works out well, but on one trip, customs flagged the stapler in my carry-on and had to search my bag. I had placed it in a project box with yarns and assorted supplies, so I offered to knit socks for the agent. I imagine that standing in line for yet another 20 minutes on the last connection on an already 33-hour flight muddled me enough to tempt fate and test the sense of humor of a TSA agent!

Eventally, as I continued the daily weavings I began to see a bigger picture as themes and ideas emerged from the process itself during the course of the year. In each subsequent year the daily weavings have taken a different form. Sometimes the next year's theme comes to me during the year; other times I wonder if this will be the last year when I'll be doing the weavings.

Now, many years later, what began as a whim has blossomed into a large collection of strips and squares asking for further interpretations. The collection has become a metaphor for everyday life, both its universality and its consequences on the environment.

Geri Forkner, *Daily Weaving*, 2007. Weavings: 3" × 3" approximately, joined by stitching. Collection of the American Folk Art Museum, New York. Photo courtesy of Geri Forkner.

Overall the pieces speak to an "alternate reality" reflective of the many different ways people perceive the same event and how time alters that perception.

On December 26, 2020, I made this blog entry:

"From 1921 to 1954, Simon Rodia built the Watts Towers using reclaimed materials. It was just what he did. Legend claims that one day he said, 'I'm finished,' and walked away and never returned. I think about him as each year draws to an end. I've been making daily weavings since 2005 for no particular reason. Originally, I decided to see if I could make a three-inch square weaving every day for a year, but here we are all these years later. I have entered some in shows and am surprised whenever a viewer relates to my daily living scraps. Mostly though, it is just what I do a few minutes every day."

I imagine the day will come when I'm "finished," and lately I do feel like it is coming to an end. One thing keeping me going, though, is that I've never been able to answer the question "What will I do instead?" The scrap materials that come into my house over the years have changed; so much is virtual these days. The search for something I've encountered each day has had to change. The focus has been a bit different each year.

From a January 21, 2023, blog entry:

"I frequently take time on my daily walks to sit in the woods and enjoy the view. Recently, the daily weavings spoke to me again when I was struck by how much the linear nature of the trees reminded me of the strips of my daily weavings. The trees grow, live, and fall randomly in the unkempt woods. This serendipity is in common with my daily weavings. The strips had a depth and spaciousness when hung on the trees that was not evident when they were crowded onto the flat wall of my studio."

Geri Forkner, *Daily Weaving*, 2013 (detail). Weavings: 3" × 3" approximately, joined by stitching. Assorted found papers, thread, machine stitching. Photo courtesy of Geri Forkner.

Geri Forkner, *Daily Weaving*, 2016 (installation view). Weavings: 3" × 3" approximately, joined by stitching. Assorted found papers and other items. Daily weavings were exhibited at Box 13 Art Space, Houston, Texas, January–March 2016. Photo courtesy of Geri Forkner.

Geri Forkner, *Daily Weaving*, 2010 (detail). Weavings: 3" × 3" approximately, joined by stitching. Assorted found papers and other items. Photo courtesy of Geri Forkner.

Final thoughts, March 2023:

For the last several years, I've been layering each subsequent month on top of the previous strips, keeping the years to a fixed size. Three hundred sixty-five of anything takes up a lot of space, and my house is full. When the pandemic started, I began making smaller daily weavings. I felt diminished by staying home, losing all my teaching jobs and many trips never to return, too much free time to be the most productive. I've continued to make the small weavings and still enjoy hanging the finished month's strip and remembering where I was and what I was thinking about. Thoughts and ideas still emerge from the smaller daily weavings. As each month and year progresses, the strips cover up past years, days, and life events as memories fade in real life. Although we seem to be nearing the end of the pandemic, at this writing there is no end in sight for the tiny weavings, as they have taken on a life of their own. ”

Geri Forkner, *Daily Weaving*, 2018 (detail). Weaving: 3" × 3" approximately. Assorted found papers and thread. Photo courtesy of Geri Forkner.

Geri Forkner, *Daily Weaving*, 2018 (detail). Weaving: 3" × 3" approximately. Assorted found papers and thread. Photo courtesy of Geri Forkner.

Geri Forkner, *Daily Weavings*, 2023 (installed in trees at the Forkner family farm, Sweetwater, Tennessee). Photo courtesy of Geri Forkner.

ROWAN HAUG

STARKVILLE, MISSISSIPPI

While it wasn't a journaling practice, by the nature of working on it every day it became a measure of time—both the time it takes to do time-intensive handwork of any kind, but also a measure of my life's activities—a connection between where I was physically with my body in time and place and where my work was.

Rowan Haug earned her BA in drawing from Kenyon College in Gambier, Ohio, and her MFA in installation art at Florida State University. In 2010 she returned to her hometown of Starkville, Mississippi, and for the past 13 years she has been part of the Mississippi State University faculty in the Department of Art, where she teaches Design 1, 3-D Design, and Fibers. Her work incorporates the language, material, and techniques of fiber arts, with a deep appreciation for traditional domestic arts, especially that of quilting.

Rowan Haug, *All My Quiet Moments*, in process, 2020. Photo courtesy of Rowan Haug.

Rowan Haug, *All My Quiet Moments*, in process, 2020. Photo courtesy of Rowan Haug.

“I do not journal, and I do not have a defined daily practice. For example, I have never done one of those 100 days types of projects. Life is busy. I have two young children, and I teach full time. Imposing a strict daily practice may sound like a great way for me to make sure I get "work" done every day, but for me, that sort of daily practice makes work of my joy and adds something more onto my schedule.

Even so, I do have a natural, near-daily practice in that I try to get some sewing or fiber work done every day, not because I have to but because it grounds me and allows my brain to get into a flow. I plan and prep so that I can have something going most of the time. For example, for *All My Quiet Moments*, I was spending all day teaching art and then the late afternoons in carpool and at various kid activities and practices. Planning ahead was important to have something to work on with me, important to keep my hands and mind busy while waiting. And in that way, I was engaged nearly every day on some aspect of this piece. While it wasn't a journaling practice, by the nature of working on it every day it became a measure of time—both the time it takes to do time-intensive hand work of any kind, but also a measure of my life's activities—a connection between where I was physically with my body in time and place and where my work was.

Rowan Haug, *All My Quiet Moments*, 2020. Quilt: 40" × 32" × 0.5". Cotton fabric and batting, linen-blend fabric, organza, #12 perle cotton, yoyos, paper-pieced hexagons, hand piecing, French knots. Photo courtesy of Rowan Haug.

For *All My Quiet Moments* I chose to use a black thread to sew all the white fabric pieces together in order to "show the process." English paper piecing and creating yo-yos both are time consuming and require hand sewing, which is also terrifically time consuming. I wanted to visibly mark the time through contrasting thread so that the viewer got a better understanding of the time-intensive process for making this work, in particular.

Rowan Haug, *All My Quiet Moments* (detail), 2020. Photo courtesy of Rowan Haug.

I have been a quilter since I was 18, and I am now 44. So, I have kept up this work for most of my life. It is something that I need to do and love to do—pattern, texture, structure, repetition, tactility—all of these draw me in and ground me mentally and creatively. Working on *All My Quiet Moments* started out with no finishing point in mind. I wanted to teach myself new techniques: making yo-yos and English paper-piecing hexagons, and I liked the little discrete objects that I was making in and of themselves. I also like the repetition of making many multiples. They were small and easily transportable to work on in class or at other activities to keep me busy. When I had amassed a huge amount of both, I wanted to put them together. Then the sustaining motivation was the intellectual puzzle of putting disparate pieces together and how to make something new, weird, and different work.

Quilting is my first and greatest love, though I do occasionally use other fiber media. I am drawn to pattern and repetition and the endless combinations within those patterns. The process for me with quilting is almost always different. I don't really enjoy doing the same thing more than once if there isn't still something for me to learn from something similar. If I do still feel there is room to grow and explore, then I certainly will work through iterations and series.

Even though the end product of what I make is almost always some form of a quilt, that doesn't always mean that it is what we would think of as a "traditional" quilt. Sometimes that might mean some aspect is left out (batting or binding perhaps) or that the format is different (long and thin or stretched on frames rather than traditional rectangular or square quilt), or materials are weird (paper, plastic, or organza vs. quilting cotton fabric), but I almost always work within the language of quilting. ❞

NATASHA KHIEV

OCEANSIDE, CALIFORNIA

> I was astounded by the liberating feeling of allowing the process of weaving to lead me. It was a breath of fresh air, invigorating my creative spirit. . . . Above all, it became a vehicle for shedding the weight of perfectionism and allowing the art of weaving to flow naturally.

Natasha Khiev was born in Russia in 1986. She graduated as an interpreter and later taught English as a Second Language in her home country. Currently, she is living in Southern California and juggling responsibilities as a mother to a toddler son and being a full-time marketing professional in the quilting industry alongside her fabric-designing husband.

“ It wasn't until 2019 that I warped my loom for the first time as a complete beginner, but my enchantment with tapestry had begun long before. Originally inspired by the symbolic works of Natalie Novak and later by the tapestries of such renowned artists as Silvia Heyden, Sheila Hicks, Anni Albers, and many others, I was captivated by the textures of various weaving materials. With a deep passion, I came to embrace weaving as an avenue to express my creativity.

Designing my own tapestries proved to be quite a challenge, especially since I had already seen countless masterpieces by other talented artists. I approached my tapestry designs with a deep sense of seriousness and an aim to create works of beauty, true art. However, my determination alone couldn't compensate for the lack of practice, the necessary hours of trial and error missed. I felt trapped, making no progress whatsoever.

Then, life took a turn when I became a mom, requiring me to set aside my looms for a considerable period. During that hiatus, I managed to create several medium-sized tapestries, but they didn't ignite that spark within me. However, in the summer of 2022, everything changed. Mirrix, a manufacturer of tapestry and bead-weaving looms, announced an eight-week-long weaving challenge. This challenge called for completing a weekly weaving based on provided prompts, following a diary-like format. The very first prompt instructed participants to "doodle" with weaving materials, encouraging us to weave without a predetermined plan or chosen materials.

To my surprise, that initial prompt provided the much-needed catalyst. I was astounded by the liberating feeling of allowing the process of weaving to lead me. It was a breath of fresh air, invigorating my creative spirit. I made a firm decision to continue the diary format, as it became a conduit for learning and practicing various techniques, nurturing the development of my unique style, and honing my weaving skills. Above all, it became a vehicle for shedding the weight of perfectionism and allowing the art of weaving to flow naturally.

Natasha Khiev, *April 2, 2023*, 2023. 3" × 4.5". Wool and cotton. Photo courtesy of Natasha Khiev.

Natasha Khiev, 16 small tapestries, selected from January to March 2023, 2.5" to 4.5" square. Photo courtesy of Natasha Khiev.

Natasha Khiev, *April 20, 2023*, 2023. 3.25" × 3.25". Wool and cotton. Photo courtesy of Natasha Khiev.

Natasha Khiev, *February 3, 2023*, 2023. 2.5" × 3.5". Wool and cotton. Photo courtesy of Natasha Khiev.

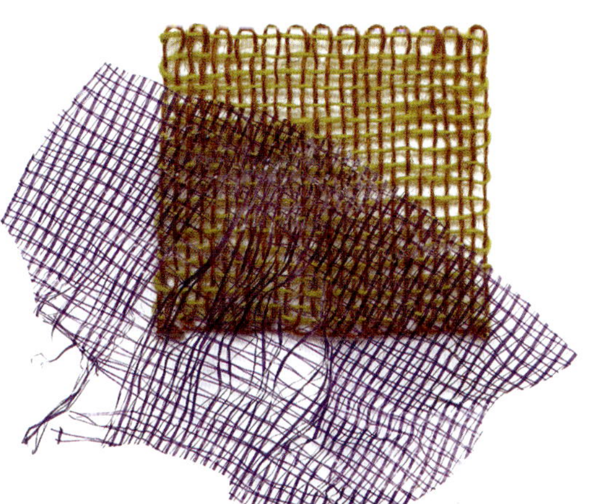

Natasha Khiev, *April 27, 2023*, 2023. 3" × 3.25". Wool and polypropylene. Photo courtesy of Natasha Khiev.

Natasha Khiev, *March 3, 2023*, 2023. 3" × 3.5". Wool, cotton, and acorns. Photo courtesy of Natasha Khiev.

Thus in January 2023, I started an ambitious weaving project that entailed creating a small tapestry every day throughout the entire year. To ensure variety and creative exploration, I set several guidelines, one of which prohibited me from repeating the same color palette twice (a rule that has been broken a few times). Committed to sharing my progress and accepting vulnerability, I dedicated myself to posting each woven piece on social media, regardless of the quality of the finished work. The unwavering support of the weaving community has been instrumental in my growth as a weaver, encouraging me to explore new techniques and expand my horizons.

When it comes to my daily weaving, I draw most of my inspiration from the simple act of examining my stash of fiber. There's something captivating about exploring the various textures and colors within my collection, and it's often during this exploration that I stumble upon the perfect yarn that will add that extra touch of interest to my piece. I enjoy the art of combining different materials to create captivating contrasts in my weavings. One of my favorite techniques is combining thick, rough recycled fabric, rope, or handspun newspaper yarn with fine, delicate wool or silk. It's the harmonious blend of these distinct textures that adds a special touch to my creations.

Once I've found the ideal weaving material, I proceed to warp my Saffron loom (a small frame loom). Although I do have sketches that I've accumulated throughout the week, more often than not I find myself without a clear vision of what the final piece should be. In these instances, I rely on the therapeutic rhythm of weaving to guide the creative journey. I believe in letting the process unfold naturally and organically, without forcing expectations. For me, the essence lies in weaving for the pure joy of the craft itself. However, it's important to note that certain warp manipulation techniques I use do require some level of planning.

The finished weavings predominantly fall within the range of 2.5 to 4 inches square. It's within these compact dimensions that I find the perfect balance between intricacy and manageability, allowing me to fully enjoy the creative process. The weaving techniques I have used range from plain tabby weave and twills to pulled warp, wrapping, and incorporating supplemental warp and weft.

Once my weaving challenge comes to an end, I am determined to continue exploring shaped tapestry. It gives a weaver an ability to push the boundaries of traditional weaving and explore new dimensions of artistic expression. ”

Natasha Khiev, *March 11, 2023*, 2023. 4" × 4". Wool and cotton. Photo courtesy of Natasha Khiev.

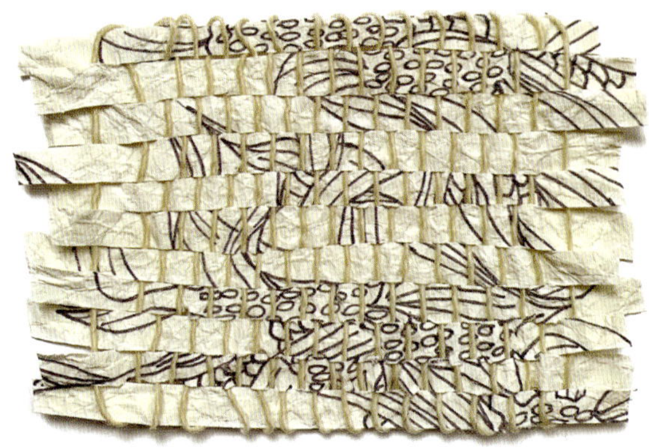

Natasha Khiev, *May 21, 2023*, 2023. 3.5" × 5". Paper and wool. Photo courtesy of Natasha Khiev.

KAY LAWRENCE

ADELAIDE, SOUTH AUSTRALIA, AUSTRALIA

Tapestry is woven row by row in a sequential order from bottom to top. . . . So, tapestry weaving has an inherent connection to the process of keeping a diary, documenting a lived life in passages of thread rather than in words.

Kay Lawrence is emeritus professor at the University of South Australia, where she had a distinguished career as an educator in the visual arts, becoming the first woman appointed to head the South Australian School of Art in 2002. Her tapestry work is internationally known and found in many public collections in Australia and overseas. In her artwork and writing she critically engages with matters of personal and community identity, exploring ideas of loss and connection through the materiality of textiles. www.kaylawrence.com

" My daily journaling practice is usually in words, and I have kept written journals all my life. They include reflections on my life and reading and on the artworks I make, often sorting through ideas in words and images as they arise. I use my diaries as an archive, leafing back through them for ideas sometimes recorded years or even decades before.

The diary tapestry woven in 1981 was the only time I've used the medium of tapestry as a way of documenting an aspect of my life as lived. I made the tapestry that year while in the throes of an intense relationship, weaving a response to each week as it passed. The tapestry is in the form of a calendar and the days are color-coded according to my emotional state at the time. As is evident, the dark days began to proliferate and the relationship ended rather abruptly after nine months.

Kay Lawrence, *Diary* (detail of the ending months), 1981. Handwoven tapestry: 13 × 98 cm (5" × 38.5"), 8 warps per inch. Cotton warp; wool, cotton, linen weft. Photo: Kay Lawrence.

The intense emotions generated by the love affair seemed to warrant a form that would signal my emotional state as I lived each day, more concisely than words. And, of course, I didn't know as the affair unfolded how it would all end. And when it did, the tapestry ended too.

The way a tapestry is constructed is like the way life is lived, one day at a time. Tapestry is woven row by row in a sequential order from bottom to top, and as Archie Brennan once remarked, "Tapestry is like life; you can't change what you did yesterday, but you can modify it by what you do today." So, tapestry weaving has an inherent connection to the process of keeping a diary, documenting a lived life in passages of thread rather than in words.

The sequential structure of tapestry is also connected to the way a narrative unfolds, so I have always been interested in the relationship between tapestry and words. This is explored in a tapestry woven in 1980, which is called *Grey Grid: colour notation of*

Kay Lawrence, *Diary*, 1981. Handwoven tapestry: 13 × 98 cm (5" × 38.5"), 8 warps per inch. Cotton warp; wool, cotton, linen weft. Photo: Kay Lawrence.

Kay Lawrence, *Grey Grid: colour notation of monotony*, 1979. Handwoven tapestry: 20 × 20 cm (7.8" × 7.8"), 12 warps per inch. Cotton warp; wool, cotton, linen weft. Photo: Kay Lawrence.

monotony. It was also based on a calendar format, translating a poem by Constantine Cafavy called "Monotony" into weaving using various shades of gray for each letter of the alphabet. Gray can be thought of as an uninteresting color, but I've always loved the various permutations and shades of gray. Using "grey" in this tapestry as an analogy for monotony was ironic, as each "day" ends up being different from the day before, although each is a shade of gray. Because the poem is about the passing of time, I've structured the image as a calendar. I made two versions, and the miniature one has a key along the bottom identifying each gray square with a letter of the alphabet. Each letter corresponds to a different variation of the color "grey," and the poem is spelled out in squares of gray from top to bottom (or left to right in the miniature version).

Monotony

One monotonous day follows another
identical monotony. The same things
will happen, they will happen again—
the same moments find us and leave us.

A month passes and ushers in another month,
One can easily guess the coming events;
they are those tedious ones of yesterday.
And the morrow ends by not resembling a morrow.

—CONSTANTINE CAFAVY
TRANSLATION BY RAE DALVEN

Both tapestries are about the passing of time and how we only know the future in retrospect. As I've gotten older, I've come to the conclusion that the most satisfactory way of living life is just to take each day as it comes. ❞

Kay Lawrence, *Grey Grid: colour notation of monotony,* 1979. Handwoven tapestry: 47 × 250 cm (18.5" × 98.5"), 6 warps per inch. Cotton warp; wool, cotton, linen, and rag weft; plain and tufted weave. Photo: Kay Lawrence.

MARY JANE LORD

TALLAHASSEE, FLORIDA

> Now, after several years of working this way, it still surprises me when I get a few months into the year, or to midyear, and see how fast the time has gone even when it can also seem so slow.

Mary Jane Lord has been weaving off and on since receiving a small rigid heddle loom for Christmas at age 10. She has studied tapestry at Penland and Arrowmont, and at several Tapestry Weavers South workshops. Her tapestries have been included in many invitational and juried exhibits.

“ Inspired by Tommye's tapestry diaries, and the class I took from her on that topic a few years ago, in 2018, the first year of weaving a diary, I marked each day on the warp with a simple square that somehow reflected the day—the weather, the feeling of the day, some joyful or sad event. The day Hurricane Michael blew through North Florida near our city is represented with a matte black square. A series of black squares follow for all the days the power remained off and morning coffee meant a trek to the bagel shop. The day a snow flurry fell in January is a white square with silver Lurex included in the weft. The dailiness of this practice taught me something about the passage of time, and I enjoyed watching the tapestry diary grow longer and longer with each day and week and month. On the last day of the year, I opened a bottle of champagne and had a little New Year's cutting-off ceremony.

Toward the end of 2018 I decided I wanted to change my approach to the diary, which is really another way of acknowledging the slowness and cumulative nature of tapestry weaving anyway. I decided to use the momentum of that first year to tackle something that would in the end be a large tapestry, something more specific and directed. I chose the theme of birds, since so much of my daily existence is centered around my garden and neighborhood, which is heavily wooded and has a wonderfully varied bird and wildlife population. I decided to look at one bird each month, not to reproduce the bird image but to take characteristics and color and come up with an abstract composition that would suggest the particular bird. I thought a 10-by-10-inch square for each month would be manageable, and by the end of the year I'd have something of significant size, woven in a set of three strips of four squares. My plan was to continue to weave something on the piece each day, even just a small amount, recording time and environment in a slightly different way. Now, after several years of working this way, it still surprises me when I get a few months into the year, or to midyear, and see how fast the time has gone even when it can also seem so slow.

Mary Jane Lord, *Flight Dreams*, 2019. Handwoven tapestry: three panels, total approximately 40" × 30". Photo courtesy of Mary Jane Lord.

Mary Jane Lord, *Flight Dreams, No. 5*, 2020. Handwoven tapestry: three panels, approximately 40" × 30". Photo courtesy of Barb Davis.

At the end of the bird year I had 12 10-by-10-inch units representing 12 birds. For the birds I selected, I decided to have seen the bird in person, even if it was at a tiny aquarium in Texas where I saw a spectacular golden pheasant. Looking at that particular square now brings back a sweet, funny day taking my small granddaughter to the "'quarium" because she loved the stingrays in particular. As it turns out, each of the units has a similar effect—for instance, I saw a Gouldian finch in a shop on St. Simons Island while attending a Tapestry Weavers South retreat. It became an inspiration for a unit and remains a wonderful memory.

Working in this way has also challenged me to think about composition and come up with a design fairly quickly each month so that I can keep up with the plan for the series. Another rule I've made is that I don't go back to make changes or corrections. For me the diary is a tool for exploration more than a plan for a finished piece of work. It's freeing to know I'll just keep going. I've also learned that I may think I'm unhappy with something halfway through, but in the end I often like it more than I thought I would.

The 2020 diary presented extra challenges, of course. For the year I had decided to look at butterflies and moths that inhabit North Florida, again abstracting and working on composition skills. I thought about altering the scheme when my work and everything else shut down in March of the year. I even thought about stopping altogether a few months later, when there had been no improvement in the worldwide pandemic and everything seemed so alarming and uncertain. But I resumed weaving the diary because it brought a little bit of normalcy each day, and to continue to see time passing in my diary, bringing with it the promise of answers arising to difficult questions. The weaving process itself took my mind to a calmer, more pleasant, and colorful place for a few minutes every day. ❞

Mary Jane Lord, *Chromatic Scales*, 2022. Handwoven tapestry, three panels, 37" × 24". Photo courtesy of Mary Jane Lord.

JUDITH E. MARTIN

MANITOULIN ISLAND, ONTARIO, CANADA

I was not interested in trying to represent what I did during each of the days or even what the weather was—I was just interested in the whirl of time and how fast it goes by and how beautiful life is.

Judith E. Martin lives and works on Manitoulin Island in Lake Huron. She holds two BA degrees in fine art, from Lakehead University, Thunder Bay, Ontario (1993), and Middlesex University, London, UK (2012). She made her first quilt at the age of 20, and in the 1990s she made hand-stitched story quilts using the poetic code she discovered in traditional quilt patterns and world embroidery. Her work has been widely exhibited across Canada as well as internationally. Judith's stitched artwork was featured in the book *Slow Stitch: Mindful and Contemplative Textile Art* by Claire Wellesley-Smith (2015) and is supported by the Ontario Arts Council.

Judith E. Martin, *Not to Know but to Go On*, detail of reverse. Photo: Judith E. Martin.

"I have kept journals since the mid-1980s, when I was in my 30s. Most of them are black hard-covered 8½-by-11-inch artist sketchbooks. I continue to write down my ideas, record family events and stories, collect inspirational images, and make sketches of work I want to make. I have let my children draw in them over the years when they were bored, and now I encourage my grandchildren to draw in them with me when we visit. I use a ballpoint pen for nearly everything.

In 2010, I was inspired to create a stitched journal to record every day of the years before, during, and after my 60th birthday. I began it on my birthday, July 10, 2010, and continued until July 10, 2013. The project gathered up three years of time. I was not interested in trying to represent what I did during each of the days or even what the weather was—I was just interested in the whirl of time and how fast it goes by and how beautiful life is.

Assorted colors of cotton embroidery floss from which Judith randomly selected a color to use each day. Photo: Judith E. Martin.

The process was to couch strips of fabrics from my stash of saved cloth onto artist canvas with a complete skein of cotton embroidery floss for each day. Every day I would select a new skein and use it all up. The days are thus marked by bands of colored thread, and are clearly differentiated on the back of the cream-colored canvas. The cloth I chose was also used up, although it was never measured. I used this project as a way to go through my fabric collection, discarded or gave away cloth I no longer cared about, and used only fabrics that had meaning or beauty for me in this project.

About the thread: Although I kept a wide variety of colors of embroidery floss on hand, I did not look at them like I did the cloth. When it came time to choose one, I put my hand in the basket without looking and used whatever one came out, because we do not know what the day will bring, do we? This idea of chance, of not knowing but continuing, changed the textile from a journal of days to a philosophical poem. I worked with pieces of canvas approximately 13 × 22 inches until they were filled up, then attached them in order with a wide cotton tape. I also embroidered the date of each panel on the back. The result of my three years of daily practice is a long strip of stitched cloth that resembles a Finnish rag rug, 220 feet long and 13 inches wide. Its title, *Not to Know but to Go On*, comes from Agnes Martin's ideas that I found in the book of her writings published in 1992 by Hatje Cantz. ”

Judith E. Martin, *Not to Know but to Go On*, 2010–2013. Mixed-media fabric: 66.75 meters h × 35.5 cm w × 1 cm d (73 yards × 14" × 0.4"). Artist canvas, found fabrics, cotton embroidery floss, cotton tape; couching of found fabrics done by hand. Shown installed in World of Threads Festival, 2014, in Oakville, Ontario. Photo: Gareth Bates, curator of the festival.

Judith E. Martin, *Not to Know but to Go On*, installed on a forest path. Photo: Judith E. Martin.

KALLIOPI MONOYIOS

DENVER, COLORADO

> My attempts to document plastic use in my art are a type of journaling—a way to visualize what this looks like, so we might ask ourselves, "Is this the legacy we want to leave behind? Does this reflect who we are and who we want to be?"

Kalliopi Monoyios graduated from Princeton University with a degree in geology. She built her early career as a science illustrator, and her illustrations have appeared inside and on the covers of peer-reviewed journals such as *Nature* and *Science* as well as the bestselling book *Your Inner Fish* by Neil Shubin. Kalliopi cofounded and cowrote *Symbiartic*, a blog covering the intersection of art and science for *Scientific American*. She served as president of the Guild of Natural Science Illustrators, an international group of visual science communicators, from 2020 to 2022. Now she is developing new avenues of public engagement with conservation science via her own art and curated exhibits. www.kalliopimonoyios.com

"While I don't employ a daily journaling practice, per se, I am fascinated by how small daily decisions add up to create the plastic pollution problem we face today. Plastic as a commercially important material has been around for over 70 years and touches every aspect of our modern lives. It is in clothing, housewares, toys, medical devices, vehicles, and infrastructure. It coats our walls, transports our water, encases our food, fills our cavities, even prolongs our lives. Its ubiquity is illustrated by enormous numbers of production and use: 391 million metric tons of new plastic produced globally in 2021; 1 billion pounds of plastic waste shipped by the United States to 96 other countries in 2019; 231 pounds of plastic waste generated per person per year in America. But how do we intuitively understand how much that is? What does the world's plastic dependence *look* like? My

Kalliopi Monoyios, *Year of Plastic, Family of Four*, 2021. Single-use plastic packaging, polyester thread: 26' x 26'. Image courtesy of Wes Magyar, WM Artist Services.

attempts to document plastic use in my art are a type of journaling—a way to visualize what this looks like so we might ask ourselves, "Is this the legacy we want to leave behind? Does this reflect who we are and who we want to be?"

For the same reason it's hard to get a handle on how we've aged until we are confronted with an old photograph, it's hard to understand how our seemingly benign daily choices translate to collective problems like climate change and environmental pollution. We are simply not tuned to appreciate the longer timelines involved in the accumulation of greenhouse gases or plastic waste. I don't have the education to make the discoveries in alternative energy or materials science that will directly solve the biggest problems we face as a planet. Instead, my interest and skills push me to make these abstract realities intuitive to people without triggering the judgment that is so often accompanied by attempts to communicate these ideas. It is plain to me that our plastic pollution problems are a symptom of living in the age of oil. They are *not* a personal moral failing, as is so often insinuated. I approach my work from a place of pure curiosity and wonder because I believe they are better motivators than shame. I hope that by holding up a mirror to our behavior through my art, I might activate our best instincts as a species to reflect, innovate, and lead change.

Kalliopi Monoyios, *Perfect Flosser*, 2019. 365 strands of PTFE (Teflon) dental floss on "treeless" polypropylene paper: 14" × 10". Image courtesy of Wes Magyar, WM Artist Services.

Though much of the environmentally themed work we see that deals with plastic leads with guilt, my work seeks to reach people by embracing the complexity of our relationship with the material and speaking openly about it. By treating it with devotion, like the precious resource it is, I am pointing my finger at consumerism as the root of our pollution problems, while honoring a material that makes modern life efficient and comfortable. I collect, wash, fold, and sew food wrappers into quilts that could be handed down through generations as heirlooms. I fold plastic into thousands of interlocking modular origami pieces while meditating on my wish for a solution to the plastic pollution problem.

Beginning in January 2019, a family of four collected their plastic waste for me for an entire year. In *Year of Plastic, Family of Four*, each 2-foot-wide banner represents the plastic they would have thrown in the trash each month.

Perfect Flosser is an attempt to quantify what a year of dental floss use might look like for a "perfect flosser" (if those exist!) who uses one strand each day. It contains 365 pieces of PTFE floss hanging freely from "treeless" polypropylene paper. To create it, I embroidered yards of dental floss into shimmering geometric arrays to pose the question of whether Teflon—a material that is virtually indestructible in the environment—is best used for 30 seconds between people's teeth or as an archival piece of art.

Creating beauty from a workhorse material that society undervalues and treats as disposable is an act of devotion and hope. Only when we fully appreciate how integral these things are to our lives and our livelihood can we imagine the nuanced and complex solutions that will move us forward into the next era of innovation. ”

HEIDI PARKES

MILWAUKEE, WISCONSIN

If, in my studio, I can make something beautiful with the things that I have easy access to, then maybe in the larger macrocosm of my life, I can also create beauty with what I have.

Heidi Parkes has been quilting since 2013. Nine months after making her first fabric quilt, she quit her job as a high school art teacher, and she says she's never looked back. Heidi teaches and exhibits internationally, within the makers movement, quilt world, and art world. She graduated from the School of the Art Institute of Chicago in 2005.

“ Written diaries have a long history of employing ingenious methods for preserving the privacy of the author. Diary quilts have a similar potential for creating hidden code. This allows the maker to work through unhealed and raw emotions in real time, in a visual language, while maintaining a safe space to imagine and refine their viewpoint. Some examples of useful code include tally marks, furniture, printed fabrics that stand in as a person or events, calendars, floor plans, tools, and initials.

My favorite definition of a Diary Quilt is quite simply *a quilt about the life of the maker*. It is possible to connect with the past, present, and future:

Examining the past to reconsider the stories that I've told about myself, who I am in the world, my value, and my habits.

Heidi Parks holds *Meuse, Pandemic, Invisible, Sweetheart* by Lake Michigan. 2020. Quilt: 60" × 60". Mostly cotton fabric and thread; hand pieced, hand embroidered, and hand quilted. This diaristic quilt tracked the pandemic for 100 days, beginning on April 7, 2020. Photo credit: Jeff Parkes.

Considering the present moment, watching it unfold as I add to the work incrementally. Practicing mindfulness and observing visually that nothing can stay the same at the same intensity endlessly.

Serving as a drawing board to compare options, to breathe life into my dreams and goals, and to record my fantasies and inner musings.

Recording a diary in cloth can be as simple as a daily accumulation of running stitch. Does the thread size and color shift? Do the stitches themselves vary in precision, speed, and scale? Considerations of asemic writing, as well as the recording of presence, persistence, and the subtle visual shifts of daily practice, become palpable.

This can be powerfully healing work. Cognitive reframing is a tool used in talk therapy to rewire the brain. Even a simple shift from the idea of having failed, into having done the best with the knowledge and tools available, can be life changing. This is part of my attraction to using the fabrics that I already own. If, in my studio, I can make something beautiful with the things that I have easy access to, then maybe in the larger macrocosm of my life, I can also create beauty with what I have.

Heidi Parkes, *Meuse, Pandemic, Invisible, Sweetheart* (detail), 2020. Photo credit: Daniel McCollough.

Heidi Parkes, *Mimi, Mimi, Mimi*, 2022. Quilt: 57" × 57". Avocado-dyed cotton, a tank top from 2009-ish, a found patchwork and handkerchief, lace, mixed textiles, and metal Milagros. Hand-embroidered, hand-appliquéd, handwoven, hand-knotted needle lace, hand quilted and hand bound. "I began this piece while traveling in Santa Fe, New Mexico. My grandmother Mimi lived there during my childhood, and I loved visiting her. Now, as I continue to live in the Midwest, and Mimi is in memory care, I find myself grieving her loss while she's in a liminal space." Photo credit: Daniel McCollough.

Heidi Parkes, *Magical Thinking Attempt no. 7*, 2022. Quilt: 59" × 56". Mixed textiles, hand appliquéd, hand embroidered, hand pieced, and hand quilted. "I've had floaters in my eyes for three years, and this quilt is an attempt to eradicate and/or get used to them." Photo credit: Daniel McCollough.

Heidi Parkes, *Meuse, Pandemic, Invisible, Sweetheart*, 2020. 60" × 60". Mostly cotton fabric and thread; hand pieced, hand embroidered, and hand quilted. Photo credit: Daniel McCollough.

In 2022, I released a Daily Practice Story Quilt Top class with Creativebug. The video workshop leads the maker through 31 days of sewing, with breaks for hand yoga on every seventh day. Some daily prompts introduce a skill, invite a doodle, or offer the selection of an appealing fabric. These simple daily impulses build to tell a story of aesthetics and cumulative progress. Some deeper story prompts ask the maker to trace a part of their body, or to catalog items of clothing and belongings that frequently leave home with them. Makers are invited to log a dream that they hope to manifest, and to make a go at fresh techniques like thread weaving, yo yos, and trapunto. I've made this quilt twice, and I've seen over 1,000 responses to the pattern shared on Instagram. I love how quilts made with this pattern are immediately identifiable, and also share the unique story of their maker.

Showing up repeatedly to sew is an act that adds stability to my life. In April 2020, as I canceled a multitude of events that I'd worked so hard to plan, the thought that I was living through a moment of historical significance moved me. I often get busy with computer work, and I can't say that I have a daily sewing practice, but for 100 days that spring, I did. I stitched aerial views, chive blossoms, helicopters overhead, a black square, tick marks, new skills like hexies and string piecing. All of it slowly accumulated to fill my 5-by-5-foot whole-cloth surface. This is a quilt that Instagram loves, that emits a joyful abundance. In a trying time, it helped me slow down and notice the little things, and empowered me to take on the role of storyteller of a firsthand account. ”

KARIN SCHALLER

DAVIDSON, NORTH CAROLINA

At the start of every month I took stock, reflected, and asked questions such as: What's going on in my life right now? What holidays are coming up? What memories are associated with this month? . . . Who? Where? When? How? Something always suggested itself, dominating my thoughts, nagging at me. I listened.

Karin Schaller traces her interest in weaving to a noncredit course she took while in graduate school at the University of Florida. She eventually studied textiles with Catharine Ellis at Haywood Technical College (now Haywood Community College) and was on staff and in residence at the Hambidge Center, an artist retreat in Rabun Gap, Georgia.

Karin is perhaps best known for her Ogham Alphabet weavings, resulting from her interest in archeology and early medieval art history; we'll see many of those later in the book. A portion of that series is in the collection of the Músaem Chorca Dhuibhne, a small heritage museum in County Kerry, Ireland, and one piece, *Cuinas gan uaigneas* (Quietness without loneliness), may be seen in Mary Schoeser's *Textiles: The Art of Mankind*.

" Time capsules? So what's the story here? And how much do I want to reveal? It all started with Tommye McClure Scanlin, whom I met at the Hambidge Center back in the 1980s. We've been in touch ever since, on and off, and my time capsules owe their existence to her. When I first encountered Tommye's tapestry diaries in 2012, I immediately loved them. As a weaver, I was intrigued by the concept of using thread to mark time and wondered how I might adapt it. But the real question was "Should I even try?" Keeping a daily journal, as valuable a practice as I know it can be, is not something I'd ever done naturally and easily. It was no surprise, therefore, when, after a few false starts, I quit trying. Fast forward to 2020. The COVID-19 pandemic lockdown coincided with the publication of Tommye's book *The Nature of Things*, which included a chapter called "Threads of Time." Suddenly tapestry diaries were front and center again. Hmm.

Karin Schaller, *Time Capsules*, 2022. Woven: approximately 7" × 2" before rolling. Linen warp, assorted fibers as weft. Courtesy of Karin Schaller.

Karin Schaller, *Time Capsule, April*, 2022, on the loom in progress. This is a homemade frame loom, 18" × 24" with nails at 5 per inch. The linen warp is 11 threads wide. Courtesy of Karin Schaller.

Karin Schaller, *Time Capsule, April*, 2022. Woven: approximately 7" × 2" before rolling. Linen warp, assorted fibers as weft. Courtesy of Karin Schaller.

I decided to try again. I pulled out a homemade frame loom (because my floor loom was occupied as I was already fully committed to another woven series). This low-tech, serviceable relic, 18 × 24 inches, has nails set at 5 per inch. I put on a linen warp 11 threads wide, intent on making a weft-faced weaving 7 inches long, which I would then simply roll up and secure. I named the finished form *Time Capsule*.

This all came together in October, my birth month, which struck me as an auspicious time to start a new, yearlong project. I had settled on marking time on a monthly basis since that felt manageable. As long as I had my piece done by the last day of the month, I would count it a success. It was an exercise in discipline. I met every deadline.

The basic process was as follows. At the start of every month, I took stock, reflected, and asked questions such as: What's going on in my life right now? What holidays are coming up? What memories are associated with this month? What do I observe growing in my garden or happening in the woods? What are the signatures of this historical moment? Who? Where? When? How? Something always suggested itself, dominating my thoughts, nagging at me. I listened. And whatever it was, was then encapsulated. A brief, tiny note was sewn into each time capsule, hidden within, and a slightly longer corresponding entry was made in my project notebook. This first year I used the same variegated yarn, a silk/rayon blend, for each time capsule; the exact color choice depended on the monthly theme. The threads came from my stash; no new materials were purchased. I made do. Given the narrow format and the way the different colors lined up, I was reminded of earth core samples. Thoughts of geologic deep time crept in as I was working, adding another layer of meaning to what I was doing.

By the time September 2021 rolled around (forgive the pun), I had 12 time capsules that looked like the ones I'm holding in my hand in the photo, a very cohesive ensemble. Once they were rolled up, a symbolic spiral was obvious on each end; the linen warp threads were only minimally trimmed and allowed to extend into space.

Goal met—year over—I was done!

Or maybe not . . .

After a three-month hiatus, in January 2022 I made *time capsule lost in a snowstorm*—a wild and crazy piece, texture provided by a wide variety of white yarn (courtesy of Henry's Attic samples received years ago). I had added some black wool threads for contrast and soon, unexpectedly, noticed a pair of crossed eyes looking at me. Personality! Humor! I was hooked. But I could already tell that the 2022 time capsules would be all over the place, as indeed the photograph of the year's collection shows. There are very few neat and tidy selvedges to be seen; it was not a neat and tidy year.

As monthly memory holders and contemplative objects, the 2022 time capsules include a nod to the psychedelic Long Sixties of my college years; prayers for the children gunned down at the school in Uvalde, Texas; the funeral of Queen Elizabeth II; and the fun of experimenting with natural dyes. With regard to the latter, one month I was running behind. Short on time, I reached into my pantry, pulled out a selection of teas, and dyed the usual wool fabric swatches, some of which were dipped into an iron afterbath. The April "tea time" time capsule is pictured here both on the loom and in final form. Contained in this piece are all the memories associated with a garden tour I took to Cornwall, England, in the spring of 2011, which included a fabulous cream tea served on a centuries-old estate determined to survive and stay solvent, in part by selling tea grown on-site.

The 2022 time capsule collection does not look like a cohesive unit, and from a practice point of view there is nothing wrong with that. They were not made with exhibiting in mind. Yet, as the year drew to a close, something felt off; I knew I'd come to a fork in

Karin Schaller, *Time Capsule, August*, 2021. Woven: approximately 7" × 2" before rolling. Linen warp, assorted fibers as weft. Courtesy of Karin Schaller.

Karin Schaller, *Time Capsules*, October 2020–January 2021, in Karin Schaller's hand. Woven: approximately 7" × 2" before rolling. Linen warp, assorted fibers as weft. Courtesy of Karin Schaller.

the road. I liked working with a deadline, but I was tired of dealing with memories, and had reached my limit of monthly state-of-the-world reviews. I had no regrets. However, I scanned the pieces, looking for clues on how to proceed—might one of them hold the promise of a way forward?

Two time capsules in particular called to me, charmed me. They both had very distinct parts. First, a base providing stability—you could think of it as the trunk of a tree. Second, loose threads extending from the base—branches, tentacles—wild, free, unpredictable, but I also like to think of them as tamable in the Saint-Exupéry sense. In effect, I saw that I had two small sculptures. And I wanted more like them. I was curious, too, about the potential. The photo of *wind in the November woods* illustrates the form. Of course, all this pondering provoked a childhood memory of being totally enchanted by a huge, free-standing Norway maple in full bloom. Tossing in the wind, the chartreuse flowers danced against a brilliant blue sky. That tree and I were one. It was a transcendent moment, though at the time I didn't know to call it that.

And so, at least for 2023, marking time on a monthly basis continues. All the time capsules this year will be constructed in the format just described, variety provided by color and texture. They are now being made in celebration, for the pure joy and sheer wonder of being alive and connected to the greater cosmos. ❞

Karin Schaller, *Time Capsule, November*, 2022. Woven: approximately 7" × 2" before rolling. Linen warp, assorted fibers as weft. Courtesy of Karin Schaller.

ELLEN SCHIFFMAN

WESTON, CONNECTICUT

I seek out a sense of mystery in my work and am delighted when people ask, "What are you using here? How did you do that and why?"

Ellen Schiffman has been a professional artist for close to 30 years, exhibiting her work in art centers, galleries, and museums nationwide. Over the course of her career, Ellen has been an explorer of both material and technique, often including found materials and everyday humble items in her pieces. She has taken workshops throughout her career with a diverse group of generous and talented artists, which has greatly influenced her work. Much of her work celebrates the perfection in imperfection. Her inspiration is drawn from across cultures and time, with imagery both from the natural and the man-made world.

Over the course of a year, I decided to celebrate a milestone birthday by filling a 9-by-9-by-3-inch shadow box each week with a work utilizing fiber and employing both traditional and experimental fiber art techniques. Having worked as a fiber artist for decades, I set out to explore methods and materials in ways that stretched and redefined not only myself as an artist but also the fiber art medium itself. I developed an extensive list of ideas that I turned to at the beginning of each week. From these I chose the one that spoke loudest to me at that moment. I started out simply exploring that week's idea in an informal, spontaneous, and intuitive way.

As each week went on and more-concrete ideas emerged, I turned to books, videos, and the advice and instructions of other fiber artists to help me achieve imagined results I had never had the tools to achieve before. By the end of the week, sometime to my surprise and always to my delight, my ideas came together and a work of art emerged. The whole process was invigorating and empowering.

I believe that one of the keys to growth as an artist is to challenge myself through consistent exploration and experimentation. Although I have no formal art training, I am endlessly curious about materials and methods and how they can be applied to create intriguing and beautiful works of art. I seek out a sense of mystery in my work and am delighted when people ask "What are you using here? How did you do that and why?"

Ellen Schiffman, *Week 35—French Knots*, 2013–2014. 9" × 9" × 3". Photo: Tyler Philpott, Courtesy of Ellen Schiffman, Weston, Connecticut.

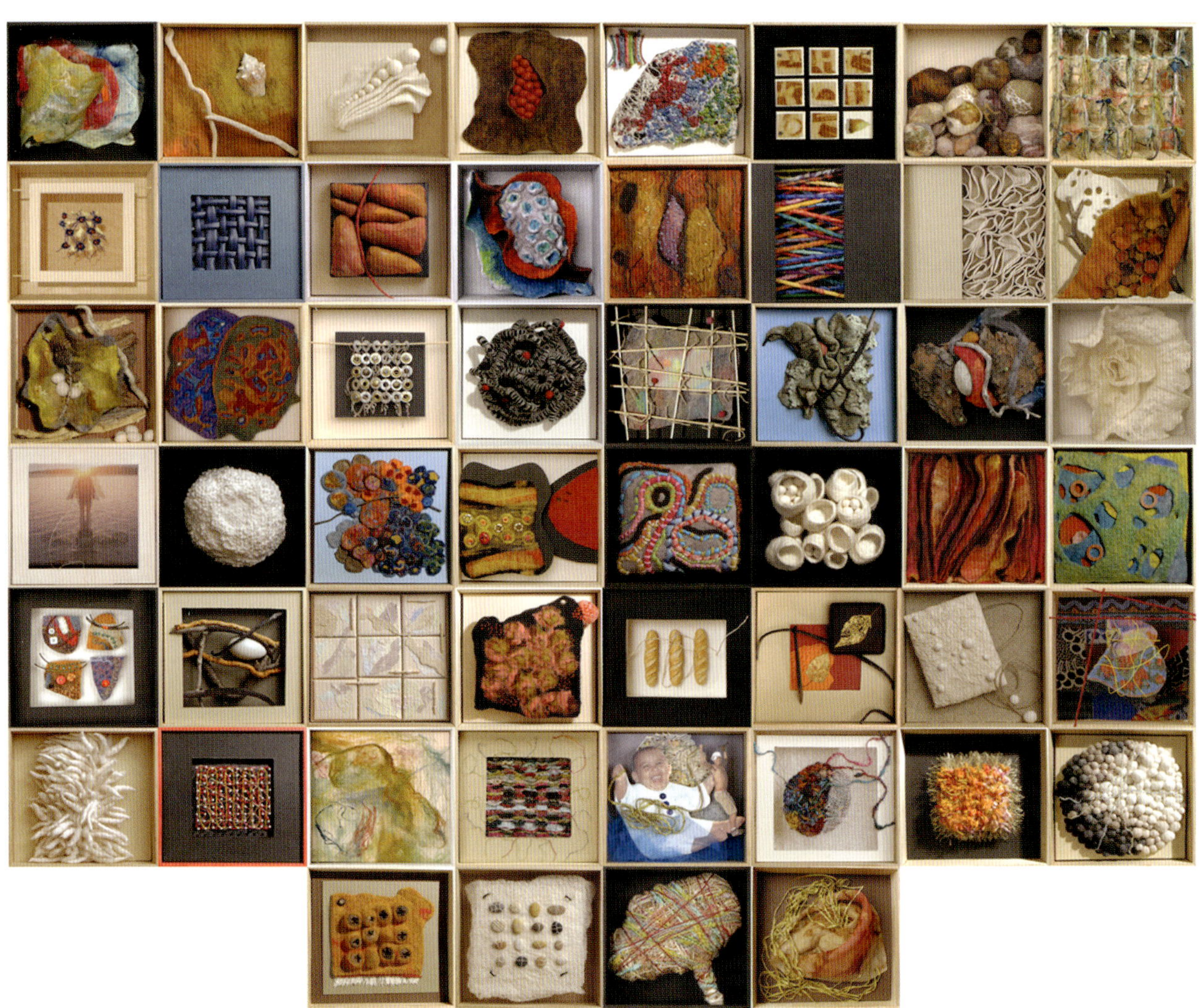

Ellen Schiffman, *52 Box Project*, 2013–2014. Mixed media within wooden boxes, each 9" × 9" × 3". Photo: Tyler Philpott, Courtesy of Ellen Schiffman, Weston, Connecticut.

Ellen Schiffman, *Week 27—Leather Weaving* (detail), 2013–2014. 9" × 9" × 3". Photo: Tyler Philpott, Courtesy of Ellen Schiffman, Weston, Connecticut.

Ellen Schiffman, *Week 37—Embellished Embroidery*, 2013–2014. 9" × 9" × 3". Photo: Tyler Philpott, Courtesy of Ellen Schiffman, Weston, Connecticut.

Although I did not continue the project per se after the year was up, I did find that there were multiple materials and themes to which I wanted to return and explore more fully. Many of these explorations became full-fledged series of works, with offshoots of their own. As it turns out, the "Box Project" has continued to inform all the work I have done since. The spirit of experimentation and play that gave energy to the work continues to nourish me and propel me forward.

There are a multitude of materials I used over the course of the year—items from nature, Q-tips, cotton twill tape, hardware, eggshells, leather, silk, yarn, twine, wire, rusted items, beach rocks, buttons, beads, recycled items, beach debris, and so much more. Likewise, there were many techniques involved during the year, which included felting, stitching, weaving, dyeing, braiding, manipulating fabric, sculpting, and many others that I devised myself along the way. Though my goal when I started the project was not to create completed works of art but, rather, simply to explore, I found early on that each week's activity did result in a fully realized work of art. Furthermore, although I did not initially envision or aspire to exhibit the work that I completed over the course of the year, I did find that the series that emerged was compelling to myself and to others, and thus show worthy. The collection has been exhibited multiple times, including in a number of solo exhibits at the Fuller Craft Museum in Massachusetts and Mercy Gallery and Nylen Gallery in my home state of Connecticut. I have kept the series intact and have not offered any of the individual boxes for sale. It now hangs in a prominent place in my studio, a visual diary of a year well spent on an inspiring journey, and a reminder to let myself play, explore, and experiment. ”

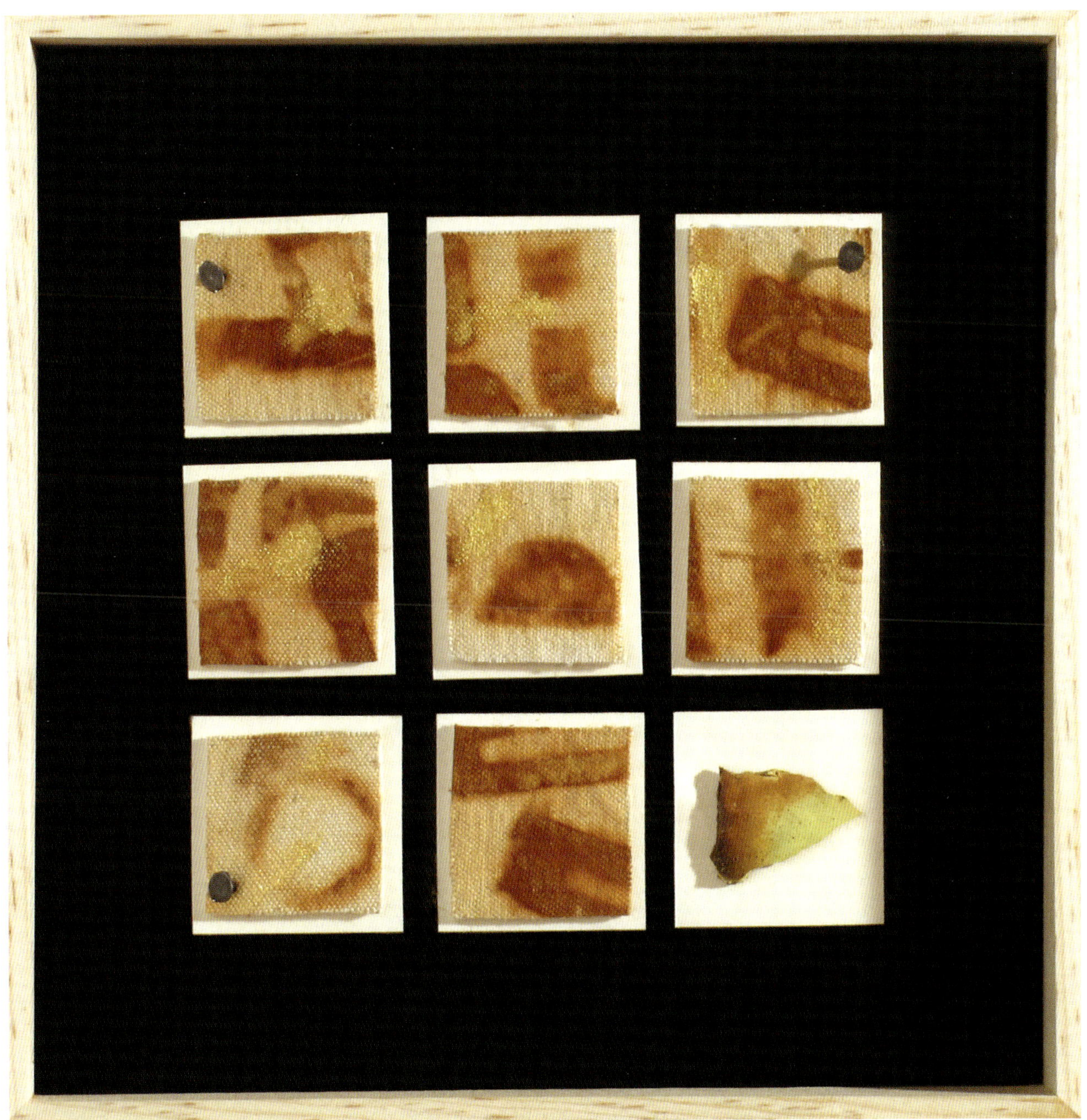

Ellen Schiffman, *Week 40—Rust Dyeing*, 2013–2014. 9" × 9" × 3". Photo: Tyler Philpott, Courtesy of Ellen Schiffman, Weston, Connecticut.

Journals

CLARE DANĚK

NORTH YORKSHIRE,
UNITED KINGDOM

I am thus able to create and re-create myself through these appliquéd actions, stitching myself into being in ways over which I alone have control.

Clare Daněk is a textile artist, cultural worker, and researcher who has a particular interest in everyday creativity; she is currently researching how people learn craft skills in open-access community-making spaces, studying at the University of Leeds, UK. Alongside this, she maintains a creative practice as a textile artist, focusing predominantly on the minutiae of everyday life.

Clare began a stitch journal in April 2018 as she was engaged in the rigorous demands of a PhD program. "I . . . was interested in the idea of a daily habit, but my motivations were not so much about this as wanting to have the treat of tactile engagement after the hard work of each day as I pulled together thoughts about methodology and rummaged through endless papers for a literature review."

Clare gave herself a few initial rules: each entry would be sequentially placed and there would be an entry for each day (even if she had to complete it later). Between the starting point in 2018 and the completion in April 2020 she filled a large sheet of linen fabric with a grid of squares of fabric scraps approximately 5 centimeters square, 35 across a row,

Clare Daněk, *Stitch Journal*, 2018–2020. Stitching: 187 cm wide × 115 cm high (73.5" × 45.25"). Assorted fabrics and thread. Photo: Clare Daněk.

Clare Daněk, *Stitch Journal*, detail of a bowl of tomatoes. 5 cm (2") square. DMC stranded cotton. Photo: Clare Daněk.

Clare Daněk, *Stitch Journal*, detail. 5 cm (2") square. DMC cotton floss on acrylic felt. Clare says she was trying to articulate the processes of craft ethnography. Photo: Clare Daněk.

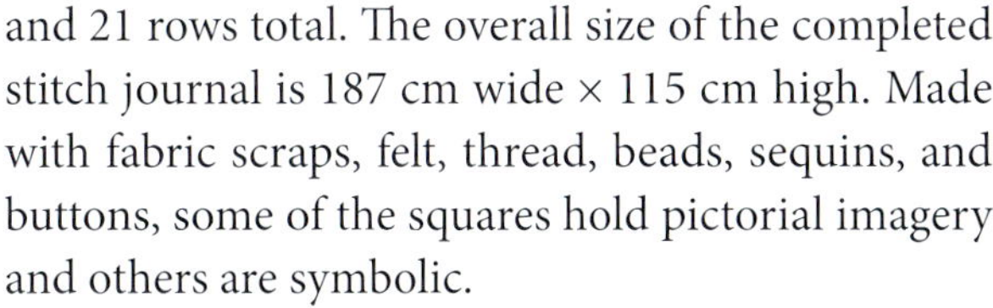

and 21 rows total. The overall size of the completed stitch journal is 187 cm wide × 115 cm high. Made with fabric scraps, felt, thread, beads, sequins, and buttons, some of the squares hold pictorial imagery and others are symbolic.

As she began, Clare recognized that the textile-based reflective record she was making with her stitch journal wasn't an original idea. Even so, she began "with fond thoughts of therapeutic mindful stitching each evening and intended that my writing practice would be influenced by the regularity of the stitch journal . . . as time went on it became apparent that the stitch journal would not be completed in a diligently consistent daily moment, but rather that it would be stitched in batches of five or six entries at a time, drawn from lists scribbled during busy days."

It's interesting that Clare considers the steps taken to make her stitched journal a form of identity construction: "I am thus able to create and re-create myself through these appliquéd actions, stitching myself into being in ways over which I alone have control."

She began sharing about her process of making the stitch journal on social media, with feelings of trepidations as she did so. "I was nervous; will it be considered twee? Will people cringe? There is a risk involved in sharing, but also a defiance: this is who I am." She reached the conclusion of her stitch journal in April 2020 and then stored it away: "The stitch journal now lies folded in a box, an independent entity already functioning as an artefact of a particular time."[14]

JENNIFER EDWARDS

KERNERSVILLE, NORTH CAROLINA

The slow and simple work of weaving in and out of warp threads builds a visual and tactile piece. It is a perfect medium for chronicling life, whether it is for a short season or for an entire year or more.

Jennifer Edwards weaves a life with her family in Kernersville, North Carolina. Though she is fairly new to tapestry weaving, she has spent the last 25 years as a professional visual artist and knitting teacher, and now she enjoys weaving cloth as well as tapestry in her daily work as a maker. www.jenniferedwards.com, @jenpedwards

“Tapestry weaving allows me a way to work through the thoughts and emotions in my head and heart, and bring them out through my fingertips. The slow and simple work of weaving in and out of warp threads builds a visual and tactile piece. It is a perfect medium for chronicling life, whether it is for a short season or for an entire year or more.

After having to place my mom in a memory care community in June 2022, I experienced more sadness and difficulties with her new living situation than I had before. What I had hoped would solve many problems actually opened up other problems that I needed to face. I began to weave small tapestries as a way to acknowledge what I was experiencing and to allow for the presence of these “waves” by depicting them visually.

Jennifer Edwards working on one of the wave tapestries. 2022. Photo courtesy of Jennifer Edwards.

Jennifer Edwards. Tapestries in progress, 2022. Jennifer set up the loom with a continuous warp and wove several small tapestries, one after the next. Cotton seine twine was used for warp and her handspun wool as weft. Photo courtesy of Jennifer Edwards.

After weaving one or two of the small waves, I realized there were many more to weave, as the waves were always shifting from week to week and sometimes within one day. The practice and focus of weaving these waves soon began to teach me many anchoring truths about our experience of being human.

Tapestry weaving can feel overwhelming to me due to the slow pace at which one can create an image. Since I was dealing with so much in the aftermath of placing Mom in memory care, I decided to weave very small, 3 × 3 inches, in order to reduce that feeling of overwhelm. I used cotton seine twine to warp a rigid heddle loom without the heddle. I decided that every small tapestry would be warped at the same epi to reduce decision fatigue at the start. My two-ply handspun yarns worked perfectly at 10 epi, and I chose just a handful of colors to work with for each wave tapestry.

For the cartoon, I decided to work with simple shapes, simplifying each image to include (1) a wave or waves, (2) a round circle denoting an individual or myself, (3) sky, and (4) horizon line / ocean.

I then chose colors from my handspun stash to depict what I was going through at the time, or the emotions I was experiencing inside. Some waves felt very dark and brooding, others lighter. Even the shape of the wave within the square of the weaving has meaning. Some of the waves completely engulf the square to depict that sense of being consumed by the experience or circumstance. Other waves are a bit more contained and less overwhelming. Some waves have multiple waves within them to depict the many layers we often experience all at one time.

Color was also chosen for the round circle—white denoting drained of color, pink that there is some life here, coral, etc. The same was done for the sky and remainder of the ocean outside of the wave itself. In one tapestry there is little to no wave at all, and the person seems to be lifting her hands either to be able to swim or to rejoice in the lessening of the immense wave. In several cases, the round circle is riding atop the wave, to depict a sense that though this is huge, I am enabled to ride it out and not be consumed. Others show the circle within the wave—a very common feeling of being engulfed in it. In one of the tapestries the circle is even larger than the wave itself. This is depicting how sometimes, even though the sky and the ocean were still dark, I had a sense that the wave inside me was lighter and not as dark as the presenting circumstance.

The larger tapestry came to me as I wove the other twelve. I was struck one day by the fact that these waves we experience are made of the same stuff as the ocean. For me, the ocean of God's love is always constant, and the waves themselves are part of this

Wave Tapestries, 2022. Handwoven tapestry: each approximately 3" × 3". Handspun wool weft and cotton warp. They were exhibited in 2023 as a solo show, *Waves: A Story of Everyday Life* at the Almond Tree Artist Collective, Kernersville, North Carolina. Photos courtesy of Jennifer Edwards.

love in some mysterious way that often we cannot understand. It also struck me that these waves were forming the prow and the stern of a boat, one of which we all are a vital part. We are in this thing called Life together! The waves themselves appear to be carrying the small circle in the tapestries, and so the boat idea was really wonderful and comforting to me.

Someone with whom I shared these tapestries said she thought that some of them look like there is a pearl inside the wave—much like a grain of sand in an oyster. I liked that! Waves of difficulty often carry us to a place where we are wiser and richer perhaps than before. ”

Jennifer Edwards. Handwoven tapestry: 5" × 7". 2022. This was the largest wave tapestry design and was woven last, a culmination of the emotions captured in the other little tapestries when she realized “waves were forming the prow and the stern of a boat, one of which we all are a vital part.” Photo courtesy of Jennifer Edwards.

EMMA FREEMAN

OCONOMOWOC, WISCONSIN

While my hands are moving, my mind and heart are moving too, pulling gently at tangled knots inside me, releasing and processing grief and other layers of emotions, exploring ideas, making new connections and insights.

Emma Freeman is an intuitive artist, poet, teacher, and healer. Through a long healing journey, she discovered that slow art making with deep connections to nature, writing poetry, healing touch, and Buddhist practices were her soul's medicine. Emma is inspired by art therapy, deep ecology, Eastern philosophies including wabi-sabi, poetry as therapy practices, healing touch modalities, and many Buddhist teachings. She shares her discoveries with others through classes, workshops, and a podcast, *Creative Unearthing*. Emma has degrees in philosophy and studio art from Alverno College in Milwaukee, Wisconsin, and is a licensed massage therapist and Reiki practitioner.

“ Part of my daily practice is creating and working in my fabric meditation books. They are small stitched books made with various fabrics I find from around the world, many of which are old Japanese and Indian fabrics with subtle layers of stories within them. I also use a variety of fibers like Tibetan yak-down yarn and handspun, indigo-dyed nettle yarn from India. Sometimes I add in small stones and meditation beads that I find that speak to me.

Emma Freeman, *Fabric Meditation Scroll*, 2023. Mixed-media fabric: 3" × 13" (open). Vintage Japanese boro and shibori fabrics, indigo-dyed linen thread, indigo-dyed nettle yarn, lotus seed meditation bead. Photo courtesy of Emma Freeman.

Emma Freeman, collection of fabric meditation books, 2021–2022. Mixed-media fabric: various sizes. Scraps of linen, cotton, vintage Japanese mosquito netting, Japanese boro fabric, found stones, bodhi seed meditation beads, handspun Tibetan yak down yarn, handspun nettle yarn, vintage Indian kantha cloth remnants. Photo courtesy of Emma Freeman.

I stitch intuitively by hand on the pages with a variety of threads, never with a pattern or preconceived plan. I just show up each day, settle my energy, and begin to move the needle and thread to see what wants to reveal itself. I work in silence with a window open or with instrumental music playing, which helps me enter an expansive flow state and drop into a deeper place within myself as my hands move along. It's a very slow and spacious process.

Creating fabric meditation books emerged through experimentation one day at my art table after I had gone through a huge life upheaval and was in a space of deep grief, sadness, and overwhelm. I was unsure what I wanted to work on creatively, but I felt like playing with some fabric. As I was cutting up a linen curtain, I discovered what looked like a book structure hidden where the curtain rod would normally go through. I was amazed and wondered what I could do with it, and slow stitching came to mind. I decided to try it and just kept going.

When I create a book, I cut out four or five pages from a larger piece of fabric and stitch the binding together, often with Japanese sashiko threads or naturally dyed linen threads. Once I have the container, I gather some different fibers on my table, usually some yarn and twine, some different kinds of threads,

Emma Freeman, *Unearthed Meditation Book* (light-teal one), 2022. Mixed-media fabric: 4" × 5" (closed). Secondhand linen scraps dyed with indigo, Japanese sashiko threads, secondhand wool yarn, found stone. Photo courtesy of Emma Freeman.

some stones or meditation beads, and then I sit with all of those materials, allowing them to speak to me. I sit and touch them, ponder them, feel into them, and eventually the first step for the first page reveals itself. Then I start stitching and pause a lot to reflect and feel into what is happening and if it is resonating with me or not. If it's not, I pull stitches out and try something else, or just let the book sit for a while and then I come back. All of this is done without any rushing. That's essential.

While my hands are moving, my mind and heart are moving too, pulling gently at tangled knots inside me, releasing and processing grief and other layers of emotions, exploring ideas, making new connections and insights . . . there is a dance of inner and outer journeying happening during this practice that continues to amaze me.

The finished books are small enough to hold in my hands and have a rustic, earthy, peaceful quality to them. When a book is complete, I let it sit with me, and eventually I decide if I want to bury it in the earth or not. Some books I bury and some I don't. They tell me if they want to be buried.

I began burying some of them in the earth after an intuitive nudge one day that said, "Bury it." A series of serendipitous events quickly followed, and I ended up burying the first book in my yard. I left it there for 30 days and then unearthed it and discovered how it had subtly transformed and alchemized. It was freshly out of the ground and completely covered in dirt, and I felt this indescribable resonance as I held it in my hands. My body was telling me to pay attention, that something deeply healing was happening.

Now, I have buried many books in my yard. After I unearth them, I rinse them in puddles in the grass if it has rained, or I walk down to the lake near my house and rinse them there. After they are dry, I sit with them and let them teach me what they want me to notice. Some things are subtle and invisible; some things are tangible and visible. They hold this incredible, almost ancient energy that I can feel when I hold them, like the wisdom of the earth is radiating from within their soft fibers.

I have discovered through the process of making the books that subtle conversations and a feeling of collaboration are happening between me and the materials. It feels like a back and forth, a giving and receiving that is so beautiful, intimate, and transformative. I feel like I'm cocreating with the sacred energies of the earth and the people who have touched the materials that I have gathered to create the books with.

The process of making these books changed my entire approach to art making. It is no longer about me making things to express who I am, but rather a tender, intimate, reciprocal healing conversation between me and the earth that I am being guided to follow and allow to happen. That's where the listening comes in. Deeply listening with an open heart and mind is key.

An insight arrived one day after I had buried and unearthed quite a few books, that the burying and unearthing part of this practice was mirroring the inner work I have been doing—unearthing buried parts of myself and sitting and gently holding them, noticing them, feeling into them with vulnerability and radical honesty, and discovering a profound sense of release, healing, and unexpected peace through that tender process. The intuitive nudge to create the books and bury them turned out to be exactly what I needed on a deeper level. I continue to discover that art making and the creative spirit have a profound way of revealing ourselves to ourselves, while also being a sacred healing force and experience. ❞

Emma Freeman, *Buried Meditation Book* (preburial), 2022. Mixed-media fabric: 3.75" × 4.75" (closed). Naturally dyed linen scraps, Japanese indigo-dyed fabric, handspun nettle yarn, found stone. Photo courtesy of Emma Freeman.

Emma Freeman, *Buried Meditation Book* (after burial), 2022. Mixed-media fabric: 3.75" × 4.75" (closed). Naturally dyed linen scraps, Japanese indigo-dyed fabric, handspun nettle yarn, found stone. Photo courtesy of Emma Freeman.

JENNIFER MCGREGOR

NEW YORK, NEW YORK

As I dwelt along Patterson Creek during an artist residency, I was particularly attuned to my relationship to bodies of water in my previous homes and was influenced by observing the regenerative processes of the forest. Though not the intention, the work has helped me reassess the types of landscape where I would like to spend time in the future.

Jennifer McGregor's practice combines curating and arts planning with creative projects based on her archive and experience. Her recent artworks include *Domiciles: 1958–2023*, a textual landscape memoir, *Finding My Voice*, a series of nine tapestries woven from original art history papers written in graduate school, and *Listening to You*, handmade paper using pulp that incorporates notebook pages with diagrams of the ear. She collaborates with organizations to activate public spaces and create opportunities for artists to engage diverse audiences. She received her BA in art from Brown University and studied art history at the Graduate School and University Center / CUNY.

“In 2021, I embarked on a reflective journey shortly after retiring and spent six months creating a 30-foot-wide by 8-foot-high chart on my workplace wall. This became *Domiciles: 1958–2023*, a textural landscape memoir that emerged from the autobiographical charting of my endeavors as an arts planner, curator, and creative person. I laid down a timeline with blue painter's tape, marking each year. The places where I lived were indicated as large circles, with diameters representing the time spent in each location. The wall was filled with Post-it notes about projects I organized, places I traveled for work, the names of the colleagues, articles and reports written, miscellaneous milestones. Exhibitions that I curated were indicated with small photographs of the catalogs.

Jennifer McGregor, *Domiciles: 1958–2023*, 2023. Dimensions variable, from 5" to 29" in diameter. Sweaters, glue. Photo courtesy of Jennifer McGregor.

Jennifer McGregor, chart of study notes and patterns for *Domiciles: 1958–2023,* 2023. Mixed-media assemblage: 30 feet wide by 8 feet high, blue painter's tape, Post-it notes, assorted paper. Photo courtesy of Jennifer McGregor.

New project ideas emerged from this retrospective study, including *Domiciles: 1958–2023*, which covers my entire life, rather than the four decades of professional endeavors.

The initial motivation was to explore how a sense of place has been so important to me. To undertake the project, I circled back to my previous homes to consider how they connect with the continuum of my life. The process included sketching floor plans from memory, revisiting dreams that evoke those locations, and remembering the sensation of being there. The physical coiling of the various sweater textures and colors is a way to explore that territory.

Although I prepared for the project over the past year, the piece was physically created at an artist residency at the Hambidge Center in Rabun Gap, Georgia. During the four-week residency I dwelt along Patterson Creek and was particularly attuned to my relationship to bodies of water in my previous homes and was influenced by observing the regenerative processes of the forest. Though not the intention, the work has helped me reassess the types of landscape where I would like to spend time in the future.

Jennifer McGregor, *Domiciles: 1958–2023* (detail). Photo: Tommye Scanlin.

I chose to work with textiles, and specifically sweaters because the material and technique evokes warmth and shelter. The project is made from 25 sweaters donated by friends and family or purchased at Goodwill in Harlem, New York, and Franklin, North Carolina. The fabric was cut into strips and formed as interdependent coils combining a variety of textures and colors that were influenced by my recollection of each place. The coils were glued and formed into an emblem. There are 18 emblems ranging in size from 5 inches to 29 inches in diameter, sized to represent the number of years in residence, starting with my birthplace in Concord, Massachusetts, to my current home in New York, New York. I'm currently exploring ways to present the piece chronologically on a wall or a low platform. ❞

REBECCA MEZOFF

MANCOS, COLORADO

I love scribbling and drawing in journals, and at some point it was probably inevitable that that journaling instinct found its way into my main artistic practice, tapestry weaving.

Rebecca Mezoff is the author of the bestselling book *The Art of Tapestry Weaving*. She has many years of experience as an instructor of tapestry techniques, design, color, and dyeing workshops both in person and through her online tapestry school, which has over 4,000 members worldwide. Rebecca says, "I love nothing more than helping new tapestry weavers untangle the mystery of making images with yarn." Her current artistic work focuses on human perception and the long scale of geologic time. Her studio is in Mancos, Colorado. www.tapestryweaving.com

"I am a tapestry weaver as well as a lifelong journaler. I love scribbling and drawing in journals, and at some point it was probably inevitable that my journaling instinct found its way into my main artistic practice, tapestry weaving. Most of my tapestry journal pieces are between 2 and 4 inches square, though some, like my Iceland series, are a bit larger. They're done on individual warps and refer to a particular event, place, or emotion.

I started the practice of weaving in response to my environment in 2016 when I did a monthlong artist residency at Petrified Forest National Park in Arizona. Each day I was in the park, I spent the evening weaving a 2-by-2-inch tapestry about something I had seen or experienced that day. The final collection of 27 pieces was a wonderful reminder, not only of my time there, but of who I was as I wandered around that beautiful place searching out mesas, petroglyphs, and natural wonders, and watching the big open sky. It was a powerful practice that connected me with the environment in a way that just journaling in words had never done before. It forced me to look carefully at what was around me. I was quickly reminded that if I didn't take the time to experience something that caught my eye, I wasn't going to be able to make art from it. I generally wove the tapestries in the evening after it was dark outside, so I had to work from notes and photographs. The process at Petrified Forest also reinforced my artistic practice, because eventually I started looking at the landscape through the eyes of a weaver, especially when thinking about which of the things I saw that day I would weave that evening.

This realization that I was seeing my environment differently and in more nuanced ways was a powerful one. I wanted to continue to see the world through a lens of wonder and not to just skate by all the marvels that this planet is full of. I have continued the practice of weaving small tapestries related to a place or event ever since. I don't do this every day. I most often do a series of them when I am at an artist residency, on a trip, or camping or backpacking.

I've found that whether I'm weaving the poppies I saw out a bus window in the French countryside, a building that I stopped to study in Iceland, or the colors of the flowers on a backpacking trip in the Colorado backcountry, the rather slow process of weaving brings me into a state of flow from which I can really experience whatever my subject is.

One series I did was during an artist residency in the north of Iceland. I wanted to work with Icelandic fleece, learning its characteristics and how to use it to make tapestry yarn. I collected fleece from a local mill and some local shepherds, experimented with various ways of spinning this double-coated fleece, and then wove a series of tapestries related to the landscape I experienced around me. These tapestries were a bit larger than I usually weave. I had a bigger

Rebecca Mezoff, photograph of bluets with waterfall in the background. From her residence at Hambidge Center, Rabun Gap, Georgia, 2017.

Rebecca Mezoff, *Bluets*, 2017. Handwoven tapestry: 4" × 2". Woven during a residency at the Hambidge Center, Rabun Gap, Georgia, USA. Photo courtesy of Rebecca Mezoff.

loom with me than I usually do when I travel, and I wanted to utilize the larger size to really understand the yarn as well as have more room for the landscape features I wanted to include. These tapestries are 2.5 × 8 inches, woven on a copper pipe loom using the fringeless four-selvedge warping method. They depict aspects of Iceland that struck me, such as the historic sod houses and the patterns the construction method creates in the walls, the black sand beaches, and the interesting windows on the buildings throughout the country.

Rebecca Mezoff. 2022. View of the lighthouse in Iceland that was the subject of Rebecca's tapestry. Photo courtesy of Rebecca Mezoff.

Rebecca Mezoff. 2022. Detail of windows of the lighthouse. Photo courtesy of Rebecca Mezoff.

Rebecca Mezoff. 2022. Close-up of windows of the lighthouse. Photo courtesy of Rebecca Mezoff.

Rebecca Mezoff, *Windows*, 2022. Handwoven tapestry: 8" × 2.5". Singles Icelandic wool spun locally by a mini-mill. Woven during a residency at the Icelandic Textile Center in Blonduos, Iceland. Photo courtesy of Rebecca Mezoff.

Rebecca Mezoff, *Iceland Beach Tapestry*, 2022. Handwoven tapestry: 8" × 2.5". Handspun Icelandic fleece. Woven during a residency at the Icelandic Textile Center in Blonduos, Iceland. Photo courtesy of Rebecca Mezoff.

Rebecca Mezoff. 2022. View of beach in Iceland that was the subject of Rebecca's tapestry. Photo courtesy of Rebecca Mezoff.

The Petrified Forest tapestries have been mounted and displayed in a few shows. Other diary pieces simply live on pin boards in my studio. They are fantastic reminders of place, and I attach a paper tag to each one to remind me of where and when I wove it and what materials I included and why. The Iceland tapestries will be mounted together for shows, but they will come back to my studio to be part of my collection. ”

KAREN TURNER

EAST YORKSHIRE, UNITED KINGDOM

The older I get, the faster time seems to pass, and I wanted to connect with this sense of time hurrying by, consciously to notice a few minutes of each day and record them somewhere. . . . Hand stitching is very calming anyway, I find, and the meditative aspect of it very quickly became a vital part of my day.

Karen Turner is a full-time textile and mixed-media artist. She uses mostly vintage and recycled fabrics, which she dyes herself, and stitches entirely by hand from her home near the east coast in the UK. Karen has over 40 years' experience in hand-stitched textile art. Her work has been featured in several magazines, and on artist websites including Colossal and MyModernMet. I first came across Karen's work on Instagram in 2022 and was immediately fascinated with photos she frequently posted of her stitch journal that was in progress. I reached out to ask about her motivation for the practice. More about Karen's work can be found on her blog: *Stitch Journal FAQs—Karen Turner Stitching Life*.

“I normally work with vintage fabrics (often old tablecloths, bedsheets, etc.) and fabrics reclaimed from old clothing, which I hand-dye. I tend to use mainly cotton, linen, and silk fabrics, and I use silk and cotton threads of various weights. I work entirely by hand because I prefer the slower pace and the quietness of hand sewing.

I was already familiar with the work of Claire Wellesley Smith and had seen her slow stitch / stitch journal practice, and I thought at the end of 2021 that some form of stitch journal would be an interesting exercise: a single piece of cloth, on which I could sew something every day.

I didn't want to stitch pictograms or literal representations of whatever had happened on a given day, but rather I wanted to fill each daily section with simple hand embroidery stitches, worked in quite a naive way, to witness and reflect on the passing of time. In that sense it isn't like a diary, as it doesn't particularly record my activities or feelings, but I suppose it is more like a calendar.

The older I get, the faster time seems to pass, and I wanted to connect with this sense of time hurrying by, consciously to notice a few minutes of each day and record them somewhere. Sitting with the cloth, I feel very grounded and calm as I work some simple stitches to honor the passing of time. Hand stitching is calming anyway, I find, and the meditative aspect of it very quickly became a vital part of my day.

The base fabric I'm using is a strip torn from a vintage French metis bedsheet that I acquired some time ago and had been saving for something special. Metis is a blend of cotton and linen and has a lovely hand, and I have found that the fabric has softened further over the months as a result of constant handling. The strip is about 10 inches wide and about 7 feet long. When it was completed at the end of the year, I wrapped it around a large wooden bobbin from an old textile mill so that it can be unrolled from time to time.

Karen Turner, *Stitch Journal* (detail), 2022. Stitched: each area approx. 1". Vintage French metis (blend of cotton and linen) bedsheet, hand-dyed silk and cotton thread. Photo courtesy of Karen Turner.

Karen Turner, *Stitch Journal* (detail), 2022. Stitched: each area approx. 1". Vintage French metis (blend of cotton and linen) bedsheet, hand-dyed silk and cotton thread. Photo courtesy of Karen Turner.

Karen Turner, *Stitch Journal* (detail), 2022. Photo courtesy of Karen Turner.

Karen Turner, *Stitch Journal* (detail), 2022. Photo courtesy of Karen Turner.

Karen Turner, *Stitch Journal* (detail), 2022. Photo courtesy of Karen Turner.

Karen Turner, *Stitch Journal*, 2022. Stitched: 10" wide × 7' long. Vintage French metis (blend of cotton and linen) bedsheet, hand-dyed silk and cotton thread. The completed year's stitch journal was wrapped around a large wooden bobbin from an old textile mill, to be unrolled from time to time. Photo courtesy of Karen Turner.

I devised a monthly template divided into 30 or 31 sections that I could fill with daily hand embroidery. Each daily section was just over an inch. I like to dye my own silk and cotton embroidery threads because I enjoy the subtle color changes in hand-dyed thread and have found that I can use a huge variety of threads, from very fine silk thread to very chunky perle number 3 cotton. I don't use a hoop or frame as I prefer to hold the work in my hands, and I deliberately chose not to use a backing fabric because I want to be able to see the reverse side.

At the end of the year the long strip of 365 different blocks, all connected, are a visual marker for the passing of time. I will definitely maintain a stitch journal into the future, though possibly in different formats. I found great comfort in beginning and maintaining the first one. ”

VAL VAGANEK

DELTONA, FLORIDA

This past year or more I made a deep dive into exploring how to release some of my inner childhood and life traumas into my artwork. Through this cathartic and healing process I've noticed some relief from the things I carry within. I'm purging and healing my very fragile sense of self.

Val Vaganek is a self-taught mixed-media artist who dabbles in many kinds of art forms. She enjoys using fabrics, papers, threads, discarded jewelry, items in nature, raw material, vintage papers and photos, and paints, and relishes exploring new ideas and ways to create. A former special educator, she delights in finding time to create whatever is in her mind and soul. She finds inspiration through fellow artists on Instagram as well as being outdoors in nature, her other favorite place to be. @valloves2create

Valerie Vaganek, *Art Journal page*, September 2022. Mixed-media paper and fiber: approximately 8" × 6". Altered vintage book, gesso, image transfer, fabric, sari ribbon, twig, jute. Photo courtesy of Valerie Vaganek.

“Each day brings a new opportunity for me to express my inner self by creating in an art journal. I typically work in three or four different ones at any given time. I use a variety of materials, including fabric pieces; fabric bits; eco-dyed papers and fabrics; coffee-, tea-, avocado-, and onion-dyed papers and fabrics; sari ribbon; different-colored and -sized buttons; found objects; twigs; sticks; vintage photos; papers; and lace, as well as bits and bobs of old used jewelry. I prefer an organic look and feel to my materials.

Valerie Vaganek, *Art Journal*, March 2022. Approximately 8" × 6". The cover is a vintage book, altered with magazine image transfers. Green sari ribbon and forked stick at the side stitched on with jute. Photo courtesy of Valerie Vaganek.

My motivation to begin creating happened a few years ago when I came across some posts of artists on Instagram. As I dabbled in different mediums, I found myself gravitating toward vintage materials, papers, lace, and eco-dyed anything. I like to add hand stitching to my pages as well as machine stitching. This past year or so, I made a deep dive into exploring how to release some of my inner childhood and life traumas into my artwork. Through this cathartic and healing process, I've noticed some relief

Valerie Vaganek, *Art Journal*, March 2022. Approximately 8" × 6". Mixed-media paper, fabric, photo, hand and machine stitching.

Valerie Vaganek, *Art Journal page*, March 2022. Mixed-media paper and fiber: approximately 8" × 6". Magazine page collage on vintage book page. Negative image printed onto transparency overlaying machine-stitched woven face from magazine.

Valerie Vaganek, *Art Journal page,* December 2022. Approximately 4" × 4". Mixed-media paper and fabric, machine stitching, handwriting in pen.

from the things I carry within. I'm purging and healing my very fragile sense of self.

I typically gather an assortment of fabrics, papers, found materials, threads, and anything else that may call to me from the shelves in my art room. I may also look through some older journals for inspiration. I begin by layering gesso, paint, papers, and fabric pieces, auditioning them until I feel visually satisfied. It takes me days to complete pages as I bounce around from one page to another in the different journals in the making. After I bind the pages together, I work on a cover. The cover comes together based on what is inside both the pages and my heart at that moment in time.

Last, I slowly peruse the pages, adding in more details or stitches or words, whatever I feel called to add. And finally, I have a completed mixed-media art journal . . . until the next time I open and look through it! ”

CARROL WARD

CHINO VALLEY, ARIZONA

The practices of journaling and painting my prayers are daily rhythms as essential for my heart and spirit as physical exercise is essential for my body. Even on the days where there's little time to work on my loom, these rhythms give me that moment for creative expression that keeps me in touch with who I am as an artist.

Carol Ward, a tapestry artist and art teacher for over 30 years, has taught all ages, from young children through college age and beyond. Painting and drawing were her focus when she began her journey as an artist, but while studying art in the process of getting a BFA, she discovered tapestry weaving, papermaking, and mixed-media fiber art. It was there she found her voice. A daily spiritual and creative practice of journaling prayers and watercolor sketches is where most of her tapestries begin. www.bluevioletprayers.com, @blue.violet.prayers

Carol Ward, morning journal, with notes and readings. Courtesy of Carol Ward.

Carol Ward, watercolor journaling while kayaking on Watson Lake in Prescott, Arizona, about 10 miles from Carol's home. Courtesy of Carol Ward.

"Journaling, prayer, and watercolor sketching are all part of my creative process as well as my spiritual practice; they are early-morning rhythms I've been practicing for years. Since I began journaling over 20 years ago, it has become an integral part of each day, one that if missed leaves me feeling a bit out of balance.

Nature, especially the sky and water, light, color, and imagination are all elements in my work. The practices of journaling and painting my prayers are daily rhythms as essential for my heart and spirit as physical exercise is essential for my body. Even on the days when there's little time to work on my loom, these rhythms give me that moment for creative expression that keeps me in touch with who I am as an artist.

When I began journaling, the intention was simply to write my prayers as part of my daily spiritual practice in the early mornings. The rhythms, movement, and colors in nature, especially in the early-morning and late-evening skies, in rivers, lakes, and the ocean, as well as love letters from God in scripture, fill my journals, in both words and watercolors. All of that began and continues to be the foundation for my artwork and an anchor for my spiritual life. Interwoven threads and color then bring my vision that begins in my journals to life on my loom.

Carol Ward, a tapestry in process with watercolor journal alongside for reference. Courtesy of Carol Ward.

I begin almost every day in my journal. The early-morning hours between 4:30 and 7:00 a.m. have always been my favorite time of the day for both journaling and weaving. My creative process begins with simple encounters in nature, scripture, and watercolor sketches. Writing and painting my prayers in my journal are where my tapestries begin. From there I make the decisions about color, size, and composition for each tapestry.

With the inspiration and one or more sketches, it may take a few days or months before I begin to work intuitively on the loom with a palette of botanically dyed linen and silk threads, most of which I hand-dye by painting the dye on the threads directly. Occasionally I paint on my warp threads, with watercolors or even botanical inks that I use to dye the weft threads. The quick, spontaneous process of painting is as important as the slow meditative process of weaving; both are essential in my work.

I journal in a small format, typically 4 × 4 or 4 × 6 inches, on watercolor paper. I use micron pens for writing and watercolors for the paintings. I have a very small travel watercolor set that makes it easy to take my journaling wherever I am—home inside, out in the garden, at the lake, or traveling, it goes with me everywhere, as does my small loom.

The end product is a collection of tiny journals filled with countless prayers, thoughts, and watercolors, some of which are woven into tapestries. These are, hopefully, something my children and grandchildren will enjoy looking through one day, seeing the prayers, the paintings, and how they are a diary of my prayer life. The journals are integrally connected to my tapestries, which tell stories about light, color, joy, and faith through abstract, symbolic, impressionistic imagery. ❞

Carol Ward, *Sea of Prayers*, 2023. Handwoven tapestry: 12" × 12". Botanical-dyed linen and silk. Courtesy of Carol Ward.

3

RESPONDING TO OUR WORLD: DATA VISUALIZATION

CHAPTER 3

> Visually attractive graphics . . . gather their power from content and interpretations beyond the immediate display of some numbers. The best graphics are about the useful and important, about life and death, about the universe. Beautiful graphics do not traffic with the trivial.[15]
>
> —EDWARD ROLF TUFTE

My friend Rita was insatiably curious. She had many interests and would often come across something that she just had to share: "Fun facts to know and tell!" she would say gleefully. I never knew what she would come up with next—it might be something about the history of dry-cleaning or the length of Queen Victoria's wedding train.

Although not always fun, information from which data is generated is continually being gathered and recorded by experts in the sciences, economics, humanities, and social sciences. How to make use of all this information is a daunting task.

Data graphics or data visualization is visual design that relays information simply and quickly, concisely and accurately, if done well. Recording and displaying information in graphic ways has ancient roots. After all, information has been conveyed with words, numbers, and pictures throughout human history. Tally sticks from approximately 30,000 years ago were notches cut into bones, possibly to keep track of animals.[16] Early maps were made of the night sky and the known world. Using visual displays to illustrate data was not a new idea, but tying it to empirical observation was. According to Edward Tufte, statistical graphics were invented around 1750–1800.[17] Methods like charts and graphs that have been developed for statistical graphics are recognized for their visual features and do not depend on a particular language to be understood.

Today, data presented in a graphic way are found

throughout our everyday lives. You glance down at your car's speedometer to see how fast you are going. You might also have the navigation feature turned on in your car to observe your progress in real time on the dashboard map. Your phone's fitness tracker displays your morning walk in a graph and gives the statistics for the number of steps. Want to know what you are doing next Tuesday—or what you were doing on Tuesday of the same week two years ago? Take a look at your paper calendar or your digital one, where grids show day, week, month, or year views. What is the weather forecast for the dates you have just looked up, currently or historically? You will probably find the answer to that at the National Oceanic & Atmospheric Administration (NOAA) datasets.[18] Maybe you'll also want to explore different types of data you can find at https://data.gov.

I became more aware of how ubiquitous these kinds of graphics are in our daily lives as I sought out those who are working with data visualization in their textiles. It turns out that concerns for effects of climate change have recently been at the forefront of creative expression of data. Since at least the early years of the 2000s, misgivings about effects of climate change have been addressed by some who are interpreting the weather data in artworks.[19] For instance, since the mid-2000s Nathalie Miebach has been creating sculptural pieces using basket-weaving techniques in response to scientific data related to meteorology, ecology, and oceanography.[20]

Another person who early on began to show climate data through textiles is Joan Sheldon, a marine scientist by profession, who was inspired by a concept that Lea Redmond had written about in *Knit the Sky*. Joan said, "The idea is that you go outside every day for a year and see what color(s) the sky is and knit or crochet a row in those colors. At the end, you have a scarf that is a reminder of your personal weather throughout that year. As soon as I started that project in 2015, I started thinking about the possibilities of representing other data series using some sort of color assignment that would make sense to describe the data." More about Joan's temperature scarf made as a result of that effort will be shown later in this book.

In 2020, when the worldwide impact of the COVID-19 pandemic shutdowns and quarantines closed us into our homes, many began to seek outlets to help cope with anxiety, uncertainty, and boredom. Some turned to baking or adopted a new pet. Others sought out creative pursuits through books, through social media, and from YouTube videos. Interest in textile techniques of all kinds, from knitting and crochet to quilting and weaving, was reawakened or learned anew. Similarly, the desire to create textile works inspired by temperature data gained momentum as the many ways to interpret the data were shared online.

Sky Scarf, 2015. Crocheted: 75" × 6" Tunisian crochet stitch pattern. Alpaca.The piece was inspired by Lea Redmond's version in the book *Knit the Sky*. Courtesy of Joan Sheldon, photo credit: Wade Sheldon Photography.

The Tempestry Project[21] started in 2017, and by 2020, kits of yarn to symbolize temperature data were being sold worldwide. Results of individual and group tempestry projects were widely shared on social media. Likewise, temperature quilts became very popular.[22] One of the early makers of a temperature quilt was Rebecca Cartwright. She described using quilting as a coping mechanism during the pandemic: "My first Temperature Quilt was made in 2019, and just anecdotally, that seemed to be the year that temperature quilts took a big leap forward in design and palette. Lots of innovation. Then in 2020 and 2021, temperature quilts got even bigger and more creative. There were lots of new quilters because of the pandemic. In addition, it seemed to be a powerful coping mechanism for some to interact with this profound life disruption through daily quilt practice. The diversity of temperature quilts absolutely exploded during this time."[23]

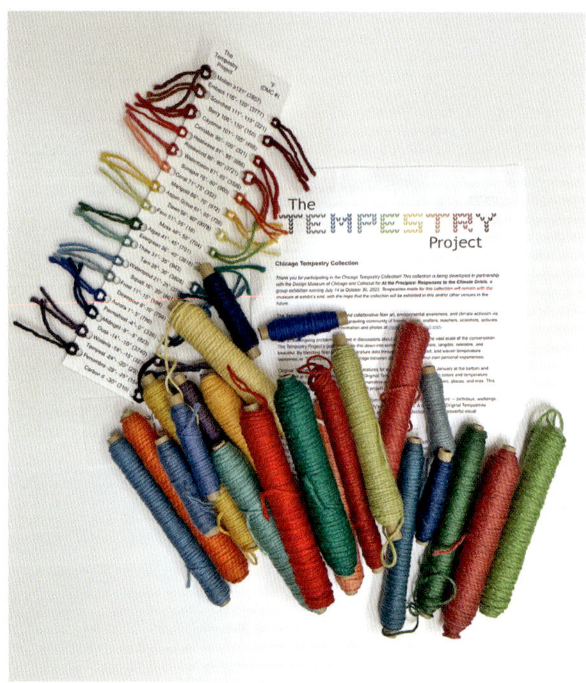

Tempestry Project Yarns, Chicago Collection. Photo: Tommye Scanlin.

Rebecca Cartwright, *Temperature Quilt* (detail), 2019. Photo: Rebecca Cartwright.

Several artists working with data visualization to create responses to their world are featured next. Gaining inspiration from their work, you might find climate data to be an interesting focus to explore in some way with textiles, maybe by using yarns from the Tempestry Project or kits for temperature quilts that you can find online or in quilt shops. Or you might create your own way to collect facts and figures about other aspects of your life and then interpret that in unique data visualization. In my case, I am fascinated with time as evidenced in my tapestry diary commitment. What if I wanted to create another sort of time-related tapestry? I might decide to use spans of time between significant dates in my life and of my family members in some way. (Those calculations can be done in a flash using websites like www.timeanddate.com.) The next step is designing a data visualization method to use!

REBECCA CARTWRIGHT

MUNDELEIN, ILLINOIS

I was intrigued by the concept of a quilt that would combine a daily practice, data visualization, the structure of repeated quilt blocks, and the randomness of Mother Nature.

Rebecca Cartwright is a textile artist, teacher, and disability activist living in the Chicago suburbs. A quilter for over 25 years, she loves diving into subjects and sharing her enthusiasm through teaching and writing. Her work has appeared in a variety of magazines, including *Quilting Arts* and *Love Patchwork & Quilting*. Rebecca shares her quilting adventures and lived experience with disability on Instagram. @rebcartwright

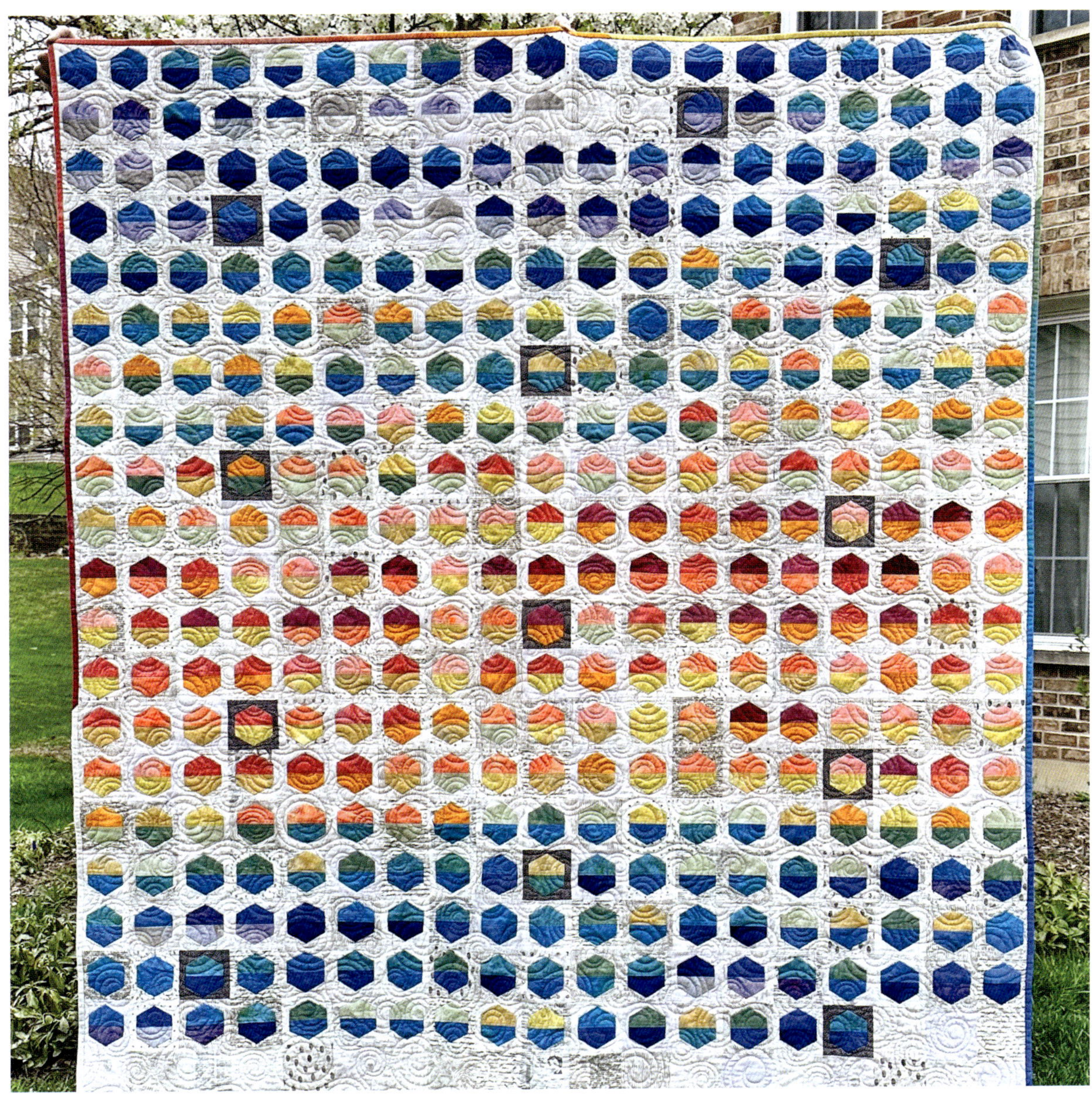

Rebecca Cartwright, *Temperature Quilt*, 2019. Quilt: 66" × 77". Cotton, hand- and machine-appliquéd split hexagons depicting high temperature above low temperature. Photo: Rebecca Cartwright.

“Throughout 2019 I used quilting cotton to make a temperature quilt, with a 5-degree temperature range assigned to each fabric color in my palette. I recorded the daily high and low temperatures in my town to determine which fabrics would compose each daily quilt block. Although it started as simple data collection, it was surprisingly easy to become engaged with the numbers—outlier temperatures were notable, multiple days in a row with the same temperatures were boring, days with similar high and low temperatures were intriguing, the seasonal changes were energizing, and nothing compared with the excitement of getting to use each fabric for the first time.

It was delightful to share all this temperature nerdiness with the small temperature quilt community on Instagram, who would cheer or commiserate as needed. By the end of the year, my family had shared at least a little bit of my excitement because it had been my major quilt project for the year and I talked about it a lot.

I love the discipline of daily practice projects, but hadn't done one since a 365-day photography project almost a decade ago. I was intrigued by the concept of a quilt that would combine a daily practice, data visualization, the structure of repeated quilt blocks, and the randomness of Mother Nature. As a newbie quilt designer, it was a great project to develop

Rebecca Cartwright, handy kit with selected items to use. Photo: Rebecca Cartwright.

confidence in my design skills. On a practical level, it allowed me to create exactly the quilt project I needed—a combination of machine piecing for speed and hand appliqué for portability.

As someone living with chronic illness who struggles with weather extremes, doing a temperature quilt gave me a way to find something positive in those extremes. I might not feel well, but I got to use the full range of my fabrics.

My 2019 temperature quilt comprises 365 daily blocks with scrappy low-volume backgrounds, 12 monthly average blocks with dark-gray backgrounds, some filler blocks (because 365 doesn't divide neatly to any sort of standard quilt dimensions), and a row of blocks representing the full range of colors from highest temperature to lowest. The quilt binding is also made with the range of colors in temperature order. All appliquéd split hexagons depict high temperature above low temperature.

Although I had romantic dreams of making one complete block each day, I quickly found that wasn't practical for me. Instead, every week or so I would batch-prep blocks by machine sewing the high and low pieces together, basting each one onto a hexagon shape using the English paper-piecing thread-basting method, and pinning them to background squares marked in the seam allowance with the appropriate date. Then, I could hand-appliqué the blocks at my leisure using a portable sewing kit.

At one point in the year, I fell so far behind that I knew I wouldn't be able to catch up if I continued with hand appliqué. It was more important to me that I finish the quilt than maintain my method, so I machine-appliquéd a few weeks of squares just to get back on track. The difference of those blocks isn't noticeable, but I like what they represent: flexibility of thought, pragmatism, and the reassurance that even when things feel overwhelming, we can figure out a way to handle it and carry on.

I still do a temperature quilt every other year, but I've shifted to monthly blocks rather than daily ones because now I want my temperature quilt to be a side project instead of the dominant project as it was for all of 2019. While I've saved on time, I've definitely lost something in the process. With monthly blocks I still have the excitement of the data visualization design challenge and the fun randomization of color distribution, but I don't have the engagement with the data that came from daily blocks. ”

JESS JONES

ATLANTA, GEORGIA

This is an imperfect process that mimics my own memory: the memories that I select out of the continuous flow of experience are incomplete moments standing in for an uncapturable whole.

Jess Jones is a textile artist and associate professor of textiles at Georgia State University in Atlanta, Georgia, as well as affiliate faculty with the Institute of Women's, Gender and Sexuality Studies. Jess's work examines psycho-geography, textiles' relationship to the urban environment, and the creation of digitally derived layered and stitched compositions.

“There is something truly compelling to me about the way that people employ static maps to record dynamic processes. This work is developed from data visualizations that map the wind in the area surrounding Atlanta on one particular day (the bands of the jet stream, the prediction of wind direction), and even in one particular moment (a split second of the gusts themselves). Seeing the way that something like weather can be visualized makes me realize my own inability to accurately record information, and the futility but striking beauty of making maps of things in constant change.

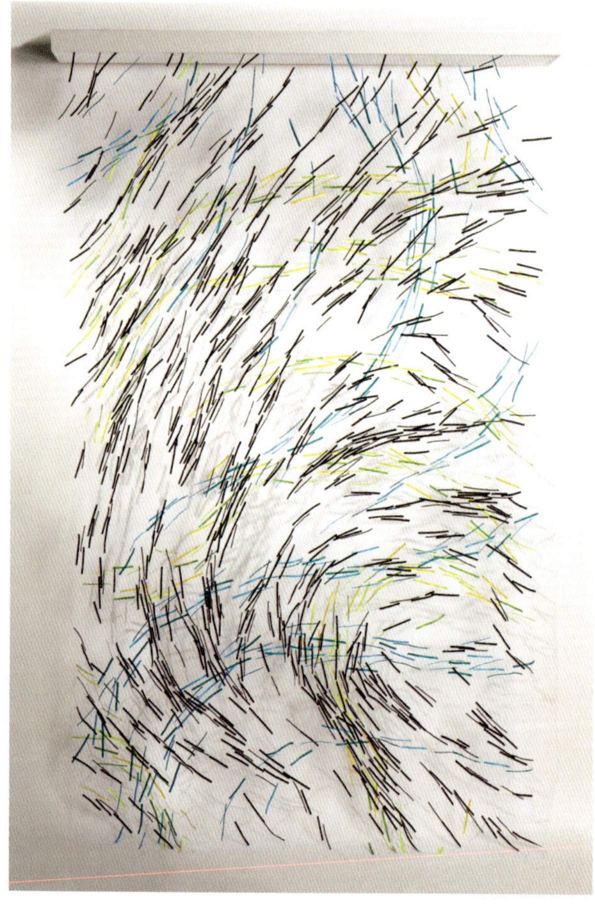

Jess Jones, *Wind Quilt 05242015*, 2015. 111" × 72". Tulle and ribbon. Courtesy of Jess Jones. Photo by Drew Stauss, Departure Studio.

Jess Jones, *Wind Quilt 06142015* (detail), 2015. Courtesy of Jess Jones. Photo by Drew Stauss, Departure Studio.

Jess Jones, *Wind Quilt 05242015* (detail), 2015. Courtesy of Jess Jones. Photo by Drew Stauss, Departure Studio.

These pieces, composed of ribbons stitched to tulle, follow a projection of a data visualization of wind. I first sketch the paths with other yarns as guides, loosely stitched through the tulle. Then I stitch the ribbons, removing the guides as I go. The wind gusts that form these original maps and dictate the work compositionally are not complete datasets. These data are collected from multiple sources, and the connections between those points are inferred. This is an imperfect process that mimics my own memory; the memories that I select out of the continuous flow of experience are incomplete moments standing in for an uncapturable whole. There are gaps that are conveniently filled in or skipped over. While I try desperately to follow the projection of the digitally mapped wind, and I sew as accurately as possible, in the end, I am creating a digitally derived drawing at its best. Both maps, however—my own drawn rendering and the original developed by an algorithm—have the exact same shortcomings and neither is completely truth or fiction.

I call these pieces *Wind Quilts* because quilts are also sewn using patterns, they are layered and stitched, and they often mark a moment in time. I like that tulle can disappear as a substrate when hung on a gallery wall, leaving only the suspended marks of the ribbon. The way that the work is light and only attached at the top allows it to respond to ambient drafts created by the movements of the viewer, and reinforces this idea of changes in our environment that we easily miss. I chose ribbon and tulle for their "low" art association—the association of the decorative, the superfluous—but also the ribbon's resemblance to confetti and the feeling of festivity to mark an evanescent moment. ”

Jess Jones, *Wind Quilt 06142015*, 2015. 111" × 72". Tulle and ribbon. Courtesy of Jess Jones. Photo by Drew Stauss, Departure Studio.

ROBIN LYNDE

VACAVILLE, CALIFORNIA

I make a chart to show the temperatures for the year. I assign colors to the temperature ranges by decade and use colored pencils to fill in the chart that I'll use while weaving.

Robin Lynde is the owner of Meridian Jacobs farm and shop, located on the western edge of the Sacramento Valley. As a founding member of the Northern California Fibershed Ag Coop, Robin promotes the use of sustainable and locally produced fiber and dyes. The Meridian Jacobs farm has a flock of 70+ Jacob sheep that supplies unique spotted wool for hand spinning, knitting, and weaving. The shop also specializes in handwoven goods, and spinning, weaving, and felting tools and equipment. Robin teaches weaving and spinning classes and, through the Farm Club that she created, gives members in-depth experience in sheep farming. www.meridianjacobs.com

“A customer came here to buy colorful yarn to knit a “temperature blanket.” The idea was that she would assign colors to temperatures and knit a row each day to indicate the high temperature. I was intrigued but, as a weaver, thought it impractical to devote a loom to one project for a full year. I decided to get the temperature data for a previous year and weave a blanket based on those values. Then I thought of choosing a location other than where I live, and the Year to Remember idea was born—that I could

Robin Lynde, *Temperature Blankets*. Handwoven: 52" × 57" approximately. Timm Ranch two-ply wool for warp and New Zealand–grown Ashford DK yarn for weft. Photo courtesy of Robin Lynde.

Robin Lynde, *Temperature blanket with clasped wefts* (detail), 2021. Handwoven: 52" × 57" approximately. Timm Ranch two-ply wool for warp and New Zealand–grown Ashford DK yarn for weft. Photo courtesy of Robin Lynde.

weave custom blankets to honor a special date in someone's life—anniversary, birth date, etc. I just wove a blanket for someone who wanted to honor the dates that her daughter was married, finished her PhD, had a second wedding celebration overseas, and (I think) got pregnant. So there are four sparkly yarns. I weave these blankets with wool. The warp is a natural white wool that I get from a local flock of fine-wooled sheep and have spun at a small mill. The colored weft yarns are wool that is grown, dyed, and spun in New Zealand by Ashford, a fiber arts equipment supplier. I use a yarn that will stand out to mark the special day—usually something that is sparkly. The first step in creating the blanket is to get the temperature values. There are two online sources for historical temperature data, and I make a chart to show the temperatures for the year. I assign colors to the temperature ranges by decade and use colored pencils to fill in the chart that I'll use while weaving. I weave two "picks" for each day. It gets a little complicated when the temperatures change frequently and I have to pay attention. ”

In the article "A Year to Remember Blanket" written for the November/December 2022 issue of *Handwoven* magazine, Robin documented her temperature blanket method. In a later issue of the magazine (May/June 2023), she described a special "Year to Remember" blanket in which she used clasped wefts to create a combination of both high and low temperatures for the year 2011 in Vermont where her daughter and her family were living at the time.

Robin Lynde, temperature blanket for her daughter being held by Robin's grandchildren. Handwoven: 52" × 57" approximately. 2021. Timm Ranch two-ply wool for warp and New Zealand–grown Ashford DK yarn for weft. Photo courtesy of Katie Jolander.

JOAN SHELDON

ATHENS, GEORGIA

Even though I was already familiar with this dataset scientifically, I experienced it in a new and more personal way while creating my scarf: putting a yarn color away because I wouldn't need it again, or getting out a new color that I hadn't needed before, really drove home the changes as I worked through the timeline.

Joan Sheldon is by profession a marine scientist. She is also someone who has done various crafts throughout her life. Joan says that science and math definitely have an influence on her craftwork. After doing a project in 2015 in which she crocheted a scarf inspired by the sky conditions she saw each day, she started thinking about the possibilities of representing other data through some sort of color assignment that could be used to visually describe the data.

Joan Sheldon, *Sky Scarf* (detail), 2015. Crocheted: 75" × 6". Tunisian crochet stitch pattern. Alpaca. Sheldon's *Sky Scarf* was inspired by Lea Redmond's version in the book *Knit the Sky*. Courtesy of Joan Sheldon, photos credit: Wade Sheldon Photography.

" In my line of work, we appreciate the value of a long dataset. It's actually pretty difficult to commit to measure the same thing over long periods of time. One of the things that we humans have been pretty good about measuring, because it's so important to us, is weather. But we've really only been doing a good job of it for less than 150 years. Fortunately, the natural world does some recording of its own: tree growth rings, glacial ice cores, and accumulated deep lake sediments preserve information that tells us about what the temperature and atmosphere were like centuries ago. Scientists have been able to put all these records together with observations from instruments to reconstruct what temperatures were like before we had the ability to measure them directly.

Thinking more about this, I put my scientific knowledge to work to develop a system to interpret the data in a visual way. I used data from Michael Mann and P. D. Jones (2003) for preindustrial temperature reconstructions, and data from NASA (2015) for modern temperature records and analyses.[24]

I decided to use data describing the average surface temperature of Earth each year and color-code it to create a scarf pattern. The color code used shades of blue for cooler than normal, shades of red for warmer than normal, and purple for normal.

But temperature changes, so what is "normal"? This dataset doesn't portray the daily or even seasonal swings in temperature that we are most familiar with in our daily lives, wherever we may live. It is an average over time (a whole year at a time) and over space (representative points around the globe, both land and sea), and that value has been fairly stable for very long periods. The period from 1600 to 1900 is an example of a long time when the annual global temperature varied over a small range, so I used the average from those three centuries as my reference point and called up to 0.1 degrees C above or below that "normal".

During those 300 years, cool years (blue) were only a little cooler (0.1–0.3 degrees C below normal) and happened for a few years about once or twice per century, and warm years (red) were only a little warmer (0.1–0.3 degrees C above normal) and also happened for a few years once or twice per century. (Temperature fluctuations for centuries before 1600 were not too different from this; I just started with the year 1600 because I wanted about 400 rows for my scarf.)

Starting in the late 20th century, temperatures started to exceed this normal range that had persisted

Joan Sheldon, *Climate Change Scarf*, 2015. Crocheted: 63" × 6". Tunisian crochet stitch pattern "Standing Waves," original design by Joan Sheldon. Fingering-weight yarn. Temperature changes from 1600 to the present are depicted in this scarf. Courtesy of Joan Sheldon, photo credit: Wade Sheldon Photography.

for centuries, and this is represented in the scarf by darker shades of red for every 0.1–0.3 degrees C increase. The last year in the typical historical cool range was in the early 1930s. More importantly, the last year in the typical historical normal range was in the 1970s, and since then the global average temperature has been increasing dramatically. These may seem like small temperature changes compared to the normal daily and seasonal temperature swings that we experience, but making the whole seasonal cycle just 1–2 degrees warmer overall across the globe represents a tremendous amount of extra heat that can melt polar ice, feed energy to hurricanes, and shift agricultural zones.

One of the things I learned during this project was that even though I was already familiar with this dataset scientifically, I experienced it in a new and more personal way while creating my scarf: putting a yarn color away because I wouldn't need it again, or getting out a new color that I hadn't needed before, really drove home the changes as I worked through the timeline.

I enjoyed sharing this more emotional connection to the science when I exhibited my scarf in November 2015 at the Coastal and Estuarine Research Federation meeting during an experimental session called "Artistic Pathways to Scientific Understanding." We had a wonderful time learning about how other researchers integrate their scientific and artistic interests, and it was interesting to see how many different ways a scientific study could be presented without losing its core messages. ❞

Joan Sheldon, *Climate Change Scarf*, 2015. Crocheted: 63" × 6". Tunisian crochet stitch pattern "Standing Waves," original design by Joan Sheldon. Fingering-weight yarn. Temperature changes from 1600 to the present are depicted in this scarf. Courtesy of Joan Sheldon, photo credit: Wade Sheldon Photography.

THE TEMPESTRY PROJECT

In 2017, Asy Connelly, Marissa Connelly, and Emily McNeil were among the thousands in the United States who had grave concerns about policies that might result if valuable climate datasets were deleted as the new administration came to Washington, DC. Especially troubling was that key figures of this administration had publicly expressed doubt about the reality of climate change. The friends considered how they could show climate datasets over decades in a way that might catch the imagination of those who were not scientists. Because Emily was working in a yarn shop, they hit upon the idea of using yarn in selected colors to signify temperature in a time-series graphic. Temperature data from selected years could be knit, crocheted, or woven into tangible and thought-provoking objects that might spark awareness and lead to discussion among those making and exhibiting them.

At that point, with other textiles that had been created with climate data as a basis, there was not a consistent range of colors to represent the data. That made it harder to see comparisons when a number of pieces were displayed together. Offering a solution to this, the three friends developed a line of 32 colors of wool, spun and dyed in the United States, which correspond to a range of temperatures from below

Tempestry Project at Putnam History Museum, Cold Spring, New York. The Putnam History Museum did a collection of knitted and crocheted tempestries spanning more than a century, using important years in their town history, 2023. It was organized locally by Sue Costigan, owner of The Endless Skein on Main Street. Photo credit: Asy Connelly.

−31°F (−35°C) to above 121°F (49.4°C) in increments of 5°F (about 3°C). These "temperature tapestries" soon became known as the Tempestry Project, by selecting a name that is a portmanteau of "temperature" and "tapestry." By using the Tempestry Project yarn, projects can be compared as viewers see at a glance the impact of changing temperatures over a span of time. In early 2023, over 3,000 Tempestry Project yarn kits have been sold worldwide.

A couple of the Tempestry Project exhibitions that took place in 2023 were at the Putnam History Museum, Cold Springs, New York, and at Vassar College in Poughkeepsie, New York.

The Cold Spring Tempestry project looks at temperature data from the year 1900 through 2021 in the Cold Spring, New York, area.

At Vassar College, members of the group who made the tempestries pieces for exhibition "used weather data from 11 different years between 1905 and 2021, choosing colors of each strand of yarn based on temperatures for each day provided by the National Oceanographic and Atmospheric Administration (NOAA) recorded at the Mohonk Preserve located in nearby New Paltz, New York. Three other members of the group created 'tempestries' that depict temperature changes over the past

Tempestry Project at Vassar College, Poughkeepsie, New York, 2023. Photo credit: Emily McNeil.

century in New York, the United States, and the world. Simply by glancing at each band of cloth, observers can easily discern that the amount of orange and red yarn is more prevalent in those that were created using weather data from more recent years."

In 2019, Erika Zambello began a community climate change initiative that resulted in the National Parks Tempestry Project.[25] In the next several years, over 100 knitters, crocheters, and weavers volunteered to create textiles using the Tempestry Project yarns in which comparisons of temperature data for national parks around the United States were illustrated. Fifty-four of those projects are shown in the book *The National Parks Tempestry Project: A Community Climate Change Initiative*, which became available in 2022.[26]

Tempestry Project National Parks Book. Photo: Tommye Scanlin.

Tempestry Project: Gulf Islands National Seashore Tempestry Project knitted for this location by Peggy Branstrator. On the left is 1966 and on the right 2016. Courtesy of Erika Zambello as part of the National Parks Tempestry Project.

Tempestry Project: Point Reyes National Seashore Tempestry Project knitted for this location by Laura Koloski. On the left is 1966 and on the right 2016. Courtesy of Stephanie Panlasigui, National Parks Tempestry Project.

4

HIDING IN PLAIN SIGHT: CODES

CHAPTER 4

> I have a compulsion, it seems, to take the minute details of my life and record them in a stitch. I am building up an archive of my life in a code that only I truly understand.[27]
>
> —JORDAN CUNLIFFE

Codes are often thought of as ways to send secret messages, but code can also be used to transmit information in a condensed way. Although we aren't always conscious of it, most of us use codes in our daily lives whenever we are on our computers and mobile devices, and many of us don't realize that computer programming is intimately linked to weaving.[28] That correlation began with punch cards used to automate the process of weaving, especially the early 1800s weaving system by Joseph-Marie Jacquard of France. Jacquard's system improved on an earlier punch-card technology for looms invented by Jacques de Vaucanson in the late 1700s.

Why was the punch-card system so significant a development for weaving? In all weaving, selected threads on a loom, called warp threads, are either lifted or lowered and crosswise weft threads are woven between. This simple act can be done by hand manipulation in an easy but slow process. Prior to the invention of the weaving machine in the late 1700s that was powered by horse, waterwheel, or steam engine, all weaving depended on skilled hand weavers. The development of the punch-card system used for the warp threads to be woven added to the other improvements in the mechanization of the weaving process and revolutionized the weaving industry. The punch-card system speeded up the process of selecting warp thread in pattern arrangements for weaving. Fabric of all kinds could be woven more quickly, became more affordable, and generated huge profits for the mill owners, but this advance also led to job losses for the skilled weavers.[29] The development of the Jacquard loom and the resulting textile production changes were significant in the Industrial Revolution.

In the late 19th century the punch-card concept was taken further when Charles Babbage developed the Analytical Engine, a proposed mechanical computer based on the Jacquard loom. Although it never became functional, the most revolutionary feature of the Analytical Engine was its operation changes based on instructions on punch cards.[30] Ada Lovelace, who worked with Babbage, is thought to have written the first algorithm for the machine.[31] "The Analytical Engine," she said, "weaves algebraic patterns, just as the Jacquard-loom weaves flowers and leaves."[32]

Our lives are filled with codes whether we are aware of them or not. Codes make up the backbone of the internet and the websites we use so freely, even if many (maybe most) of us cannot do computer

Karin Schaller, *Brigit Chill Dara* (detail), one of *Sanctuary Curtains: Ogham Alphabet* series of weavings, circa 1994–1996. Woven: 41.25" × 21.5". Silk/rayon, cotton, and metallic threads, Summer and Winter technique with pickup in areas. Courtesy of Karin Schaller.

coding. Almost every product we buy has a UPC (Universal Product Code) 12-digit number identifying the product and vendor, and a corresponding barcode, patterns of black and white lines, that an optical scanner reads. These track items for business inventory and retail checkout. We often scan QR (Quick Response) codes, a square made up of differing arrangements of many smaller black and white squares, to be directed to a website. But more basic than that, perhaps we're using a form of code each time we put pen to paper. After all, shouldn't we also consider the systems of writing that we learn as children to be codes? A *Guardian* article states,

> When no one is left who knows how to read a language, it becomes a secret code of its own. That is exactly what happened with the hieroglyphs of ancient Egypt. These beautiful, iconic characters baffled linguists for centuries, until Napoleon's troops discovered the Rosetta Stone, which allowed scholars to match the hieroglyphs with known Greek words, giving us the key to understanding the language and culture of one of the greatest civilizations in history.[33]

Over the centuries, different scripts or writing systems have developed. Many ancient ones have been deciphered, while others await unlocking. These different scripts or writing systems have motivated some artists to adapt them in their artwork. One example is the Ogham alphabet, found on stone monuments in parts of Britain dating back to at least the fourth century. The origin of Ogham is not certain, but it was possibly invented by Irish speakers to hide messages from Roman Britain or by early Christians to record primitive Irish.[34] Karin Schaller, whose *Time Capsules* are shown in another part of this book, was earlier inspired by the Ogham alphabet to create a series of weavings.

Michael Rohde is another artist who has created a series of weavings he calls Imagined Languages: "I imagined a new language and represented it in tapestry that might also be seen as a computer code. Rather than expecting the units of each to be a word-by-word message, color choices and pattern arrangement symbolically convey the concept named in each title."

Many other codes exist. Morse code, for instance, was developed in the 19th century; its electrical coding system transmitted information using a series of dots, dashes, and gaps.[35] Also created in the 19th century, Braille is a tactile coding system that allows visually impaired people access to written information. Braille uses patterns of raised dots to represent letters of the alphabet as well as numerals.

Early examples of information coded in textiles are found in the Inca quipu (khipu), knotted cords that were probably used as accounting records and for other information. Dating from 1400 to 1532 CE, over 600 of the quipu have survived because of the dry climate conditions in the southern coastal area of Peru where they were found.[36] Information was recorded in the cords by a system of knots and the numbers and colors of cords.

Hiding information in plain sight through steganography has also had many uses. Steganography is the practice of concealing messages or information within other nonsecret text or data. Jordan Cunliffe described how she used steganography in her artwork to hide very personal information as she stitched: "I was working in this way before I even knew the word."

Steganography was also used in wartime. In *A Guide to Codes and Signals,* written in 1942, the authors state,

> Spies have been known to work code messages into knitting, embroidery, hooked rugs, and so on. Small knots are tied at certain intervals in the thread or yarn. When unraveled, the thread is placed alongside a decoder and the spacing of the knots reveals the letters of the secret message. In Charles Dickens's novel *A Tale of Two Cities*, Madame LaFarge knitted industriously most of the time. She was working into her knitting the names of all those destined for the guillotine when the revolution began.[37]

Sally Coulthard, in her book *A Short History of the World According to Sheep*, mentions several examples of knitting being used as a cover for passing information. She describes how legend says Molly Rinker, a tavern owner during the American Revolution, would overhear conversations by British occupiers in Philadelphia when their "tongues had been loosened by alcohol." She would take note of enemy strategy, wrap her notes in balls of wool, and drop them over the edge of a cliff as she sat knitting the next day—right into the hands of a colonial dispatch rider.

Coulthard also states that the use of knitting to transmit coded information was taken so seriously in World War II that the US Office of Censorship banned knitting patterns from being posted abroad, just in case there was coded information being provided.[38]

Michael F. Rohde. *Florid*, one of the *Imagined Languages* tapestries, in process on the loom, 2020. Handwoven tapestry: 76" × 49". Wool, camel, goat, mohair, natural dyes. Photo courtesy of Michael F. Rohde.

Weavers have long transmitted pattern information though weaving drafts, a shorthand way of representing how warp and weft threads will interact in a pattern. An introduction to "reading" the code of weaving drafts usually comes when learning the craft. Occasionally, weavers use "name drafting" or "code drafting" to create personalized designs on their looms.[39] The idea is not a new one—in a 1942 article, "Designing Your Own Name Pattern Drafts" in *Handweaving News,* the author Nellie Sargent Johnson states that the method wasn't original to her.

Name drafting is a way to create unique designs more complex than basic plain weave (over one, under one as weft covers warp). Following the sequence determined by the name draft, different frames or shafts on the loom are threaded with the warp. The combination of shafts designed in the draft and the order of their use cause the pattern to develop as the cloth is woven. With name drafting, one can encode letters of the alphabet and numbers 0 to 9 to create an original design that holds special, personalized meaning.[40]

Several artists featured in this book have used the concept of codes in their artwork. Kay Lawrence, whose tapestry diary was mentioned earlier, assigned values of gray to signify letters of the alphabet and, with those, encoded the words of a poem as she wove a small tapestry, *Monotony*. Recently, inspired by this idea, I created a code of colors for the alphabet and wove a small tapestry using the words of Emily Dickinson's poem "'Hope' is the thing with feathers." Susan Martin Maffei employed quipu in her tapestries *Nessa Nessa, Winter Moon* and *Alvia Jane* to record personal details about her family members. In my own work, I have woven textured dots in Braille to sign and date my first yearlong tapestry diary.

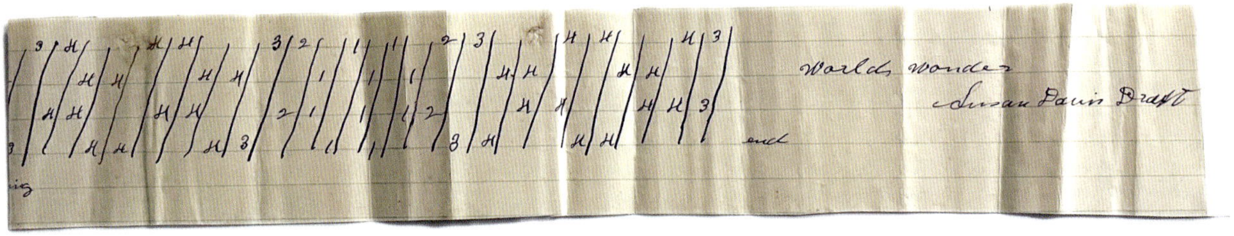

Weaving draft. Paper. Lorenzo Dow Davis Collection. Chestatee Regional Library, Lumpkin County Genealogy and Archives, Dahlonega, Georgia. Photo: Tommye Scanlin.

Archie Brennan, *Sonnet without Words*, 2006. Handwoven tapestry: 40" × 25". Courtesy of Christine Elizabeth Humphrys.

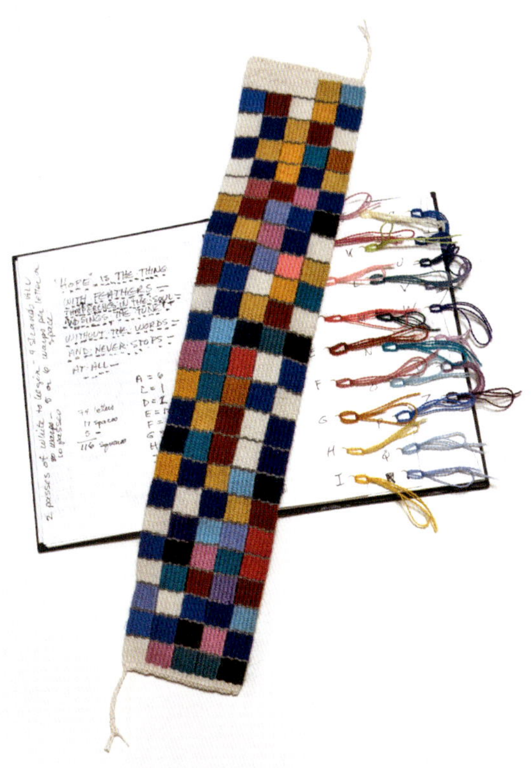

Tommye Scanlin, *Hope is the Thing with Feathers . . .*, 2023. Handwoven tapestry: 18" × 3.5". Wool and cotton. An alphabet code was designed using 26 different colors. The letters for words of Emily Dickinson's poem were chosen for each square, corresponding to the self-determined code. Photo: Chris Dant.

In 2011 I was in a workshop with Archie Brennan and Susan Martin Maffei, during which time he mentioned a tapestry that he designed by using a deck of cards and the line structure of a sonnet. He described it as an "open journey of the process." This idea expanded upon a concept he and Susan had been using in workshops in which participants used a deck of playing cards to select color and width of bands of color.

In the tapestry, Archie decided to use the sonnet form of 16 lines (title, six-line verse, and eight-line verse). Using this idea, he marked off 16 horizontal lines on the warp. He selected 30 cards from a deck of cards: 26 for the alphabet and four blanks to define word length. For the alphabet cards he designated basic geometric shapes to weave, cutting the cards to weave whatever shape turned up. For the background he chose neutral color, with other colors chosen from a smaller deck of 12 cards representing 12 predetermined hues.

"I followed the rules, strictly weaving the colors, letter shapes, and spaces that were determined by the cards, from left to right and bottom to top, and I accepted the result: A Sonnet without Words."[41]

Hearing Archie talk about his *Sonnet without Words* at the workshop inspired me to try using chance in some way to design a tapestry. Later that summer I began to use the roll of a die for planning shapes and colors in a small weaving, an idea I've used several times over through the years.

Tommye Scanlin, tapestry with design selected by throw of a die. Photo: Tommye Scanlin.

There are many creative ways to incorporate ideas from existing code systems, and I have mentioned only a few. Knots, stitches, fabric pieces in contrasting colors, woven shapes to create symbols—each of those techniques could give starting places for exploring codes in your own ways by using existing ones or devising your own.

SUSAN MARTIN MAFFEI

NEW BALTIMORE, NEW YORK

Observation is my daily practice and journaling is my weaving those into visual forms using fiber as my medium whether techniques of tapestry, crochet, or book arts and constructions.

Susan Martin Maffei is a fiber artist working primarily in tapestry. Her studies include studio work at the Art Students League NYC, and apprenticeships at Scheuer Tapestry Studio NYC and Perfection of Tapestry Techniques at Les Gobelins in Paris, France. She has taught and exhibited in North America and abroad in Europe, Australia, and New Zealand. She has works both in private and public collections. She maintains a studio in upstate New York.

"Observation is my daily practice, and journaling is my weaving those observations into visual forms using fiber as my medium, whether techniques of tapestry, crochet, or book arts and constructions.

Fiber has been an essential part of my life since I was a child, and I learned early the sensual tactile nature of fiber making through my grandmother, an accomplished needleworker. It is my preferred method of expression and through practice and historical study has led me on a most satisfying journey of discovery and fiber language.

Once an interesting occasion triggers a vision, I have a tendency to chew on it for quite a while, perhaps doing some research, perhaps a sample of what I think is an appropriate fiber and technique. I might do a series of small sketches to clarify my vision. Then I simply start, and as the idea grows I add and subtract depending on how its language is building. Not all projects result in a successful ending and that is what keeps me making.

Susan Martin Maffei, *Nessa Nessa Winter Moon*, 2014. Handwoven tapestry and mixed media: 252" full length; 20" × 9" × 8" when closed. Tapestry is handspun wool warp, indigo-dyed silks, Bulgarian silks, wool, linen, hemp, cotton and metallic wefts. Mount is acid-free book board, fabric, acid-free Canson paper and glues. The tapestry is mounted on a series of 28 screens arranged as an accordion book. It can be viewed in many ways—circular, accordion, or stretched out to its full length. When closed, it is a compact large book.

Much like the history of the book that develops from scrolls into accordion book form, the work *Nessa Nessa, Winter Moon* combines tapestry with book arts and adds an additional third dimension by the use of the ancient Andean khipu (or quipu). A quipu is a unique system expressed on a spatial array of colored knotted cords that was used by cultures such as Huari (ca. 500–800 CE) and Inca (ca. 1400–1535 CE) in pre-Columbian Peru to record and transmit information.

In *Nessa Nessa, Winter Moon*, I used quipu to note the time of the rising and setting of the moon and the moon phases over the Hudson for an entire year. It begins with an eclipse that occurs on the winter solstice.

The narrative panels of the woven tapestry include a legend, calendar, important constellations in the months they are best viewed, and daily azimuth of the rising and setting moon, as well as changes in light and weather, and scenes of ships and tugs

Susan Martin Maffei, *Nessa Nessa Winter Moon* (open, two-page spread—18" across). Handwoven tapestry and mixed media: 252" full length; 20" × 9" × 8" when closed. Tapestry is handspun wool warp, indigo-dyed silks, Bulgarian silks, wool, linen, hemp, cotton and metallic wefts.

passing on the river over an average 24-hour period in winter. The title is taken from a Native American song dedicated to the winter grandmother moon, and occupies one of the last panels, with native flute notations. The tapestry ends with my mother's dog and me playing tribute to the full moon.

The inspiration for the work was multipart, and included moving to a small hamlet on the Hudson River and watching the changing landscape each day. Another inspiration was the eclipse of the full moon that happened to occur on my mother's birthday just a year after her passing. My continuing interest in the quipu as a form of textile language and a recent foray into the making and history of book arts added to the motivation for the work.

The tapestry is mounted on a series of 28 panels in accordion book form that can be viewed in many ways: circular, accordion, or stretched out to a full length of 252 inches. When closed, it is a large compact book, 20 inches high × 9 inches wide × 8 inches deep.

Its materials are handspun wool warp and quipu, indigo-dyed silks, Bulgarian silk, wool, linen, cotton,

Susan Martin Maffei, *Nessa Nessa Winter Moon* (closed). Handwoven tapestry and mixed media: 20" × 9" × 8" when closed.

hemp, and metallic weft. Book materials are acid-free book board, book cloth, Canson papers, glue, and thread.

The quipu used in *Alvia Jane* records the genealogy of the Disbrow and Martin families, maternal and paternal sides, which have each contributed their genes to *Alvia Jane* (a self-portrait). The quipu is read from the middle, starting with the only salmon-and-white-combined cord (representing me). Disbrows (maternal ancestors) are on the left and Martins (paternal) on the right. Direct male ancestors are represented as white cords. Siblings of direct ancestor males are represented in black for males and salmon for females. The two gold cords represent my grandmothers. The ply of each cord represents the gender of the ancestor, S-plied for male and Z-plied for female. Each generation is separated by a space on the main supporting cord. Each cord contains the year of birth and subsidiary cords contain the year of death. (Some cords are missing dates yet to be researched and are therefore blank.) The dates are read from the top of the cord down, and each knot represents a number. The digits are represented as a special looped knot.

Quipus were often found accompanied by a group of black and white stones. It is believed that these stones assisted in some form of binary language that helped the reader decipher the knots. The accompanying stones used with the artwork have been collected from the property that has belonged to the Disbrow family for hundreds of years and now carries the names of the descendants. ”

Susan Martin Maffei, *Alvia Jane* (detail of quipu).

Susan Martin Maffei, *Alvia Jane*, 2007. Handwoven tapestry and mixed media: 40" × 45" plus quipu and stones. Cotton warp, wool weft, and quipu.

MICHAEL ROHDE

WESTLAKE VILLAGE, CALIFORNIA

Often I've been intrigued by the idea of representing text or language in tapestry; several earlier ones of mine emulated Tibetan prayer flag inscriptions, but as lines of short and long dashes that might approximate the original Tibetan printed prayers on the flags.

Michael Rohde has been weaving since 1973. His formal training in drawing, color, and design was at the Alfred Glassel School of the Houston Museum of Fine Arts. His work has been widely exhibited nationally and internationally and is in the permanent collections of many museums around the country, including the Textile Museum (Washington, DC) and the Art Institute of Chicago.

“Often I've been intrigued by the idea of representing text or language in tapestry; several earlier ones of mine emulated Tibetan prayer flag inscriptions, but as lines of short and long dashes that might approximate the original Tibetan printed prayers on the flags.

The genesis of the series of tapestries presented here started with ideas I'd encountered in talks and writings by scholars such as Mary Frame. She posited that repeated imagery in Inca-era textiles might be

Michael F. Rohde, *Mysterious* (detail), 2020. Handwoven tapestry: 77" × 48.5". Wool, camel, natural dyes. Photo credit: W. Scott Miles.

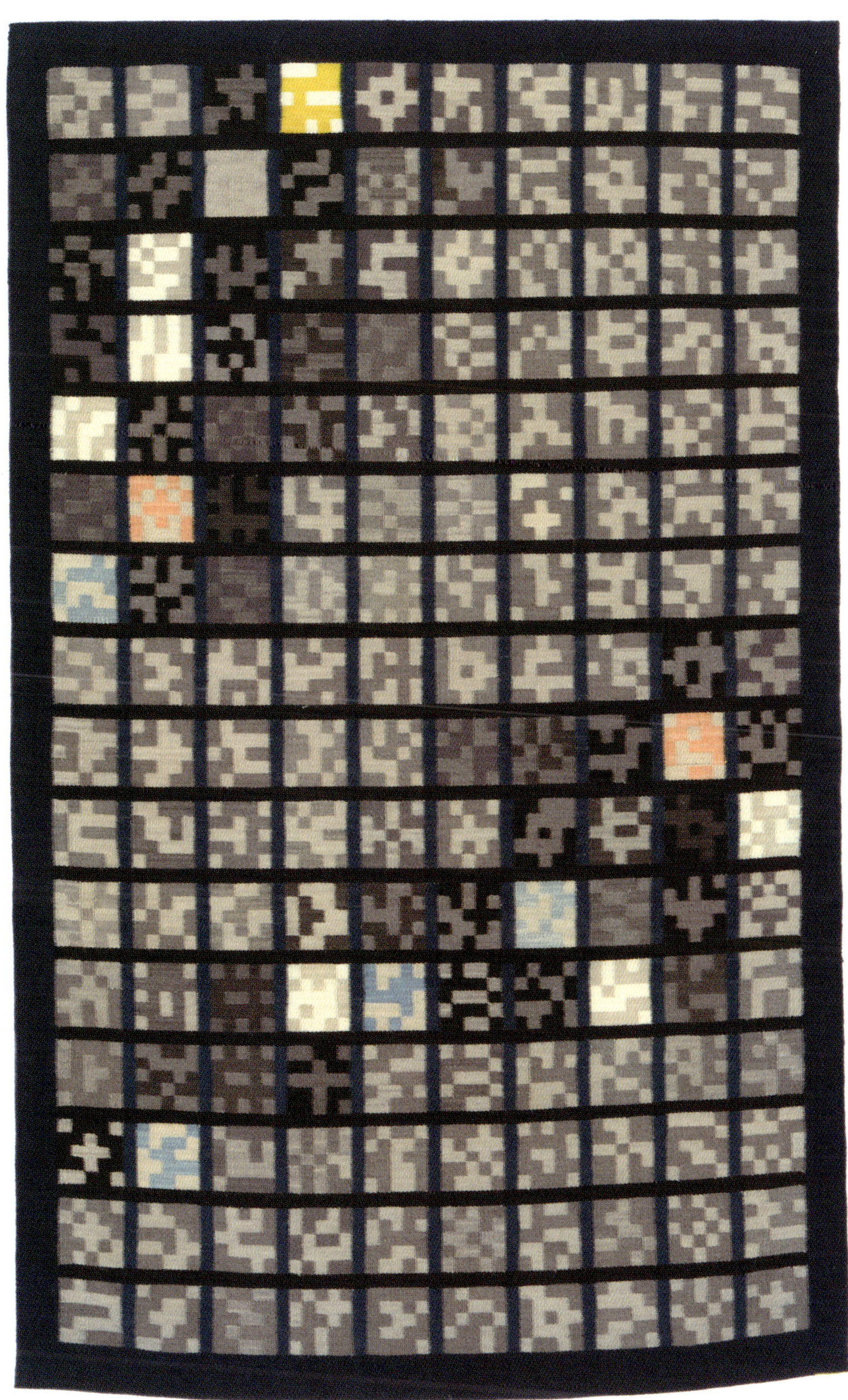

Michael F. Rohde, *Illuminative*, 2020. Handwoven tapestry: 77" × 48". Cotton and wool, hand-dyed with natural dyes. Photo credit: W. Scott Miles.

of an undeciphered language.

When I considered how to adapt this concept in my own tapestry designs, my first thought was to create a series of blocks made up of 25 smaller blocks. These were the units of the Imagined Language. A couple hundred variations of these two-color patterns were generated. Each one could be thought of as letters, words, or ideas.

Although arranged in a table of 10 by 16 blocks, the content of each block and the order in which they are presented have no linguistic meaning, since they were chosen at random from the pool of created blocks. Rather, the set of color choices for each tapestry stood in as a message, symbolically. *Mysterious* reflects on some political speech and uses purples, grays, and hard-to-classify shades of yellow-tans. *Illuminative* considers desires for guidance in speech; the constellations Ursa Major and Minor are approximated, with the North Star a prominent yellow at the top. All of my wool is dyed with natural dyes.

As I considered the finished piece, it was rather obvious that this presentation of blocks of pattern could be likened to computer codes, such as QR symbols; briefly I wondered if a QR code reader might take the viewer to an unexpected website? ❞

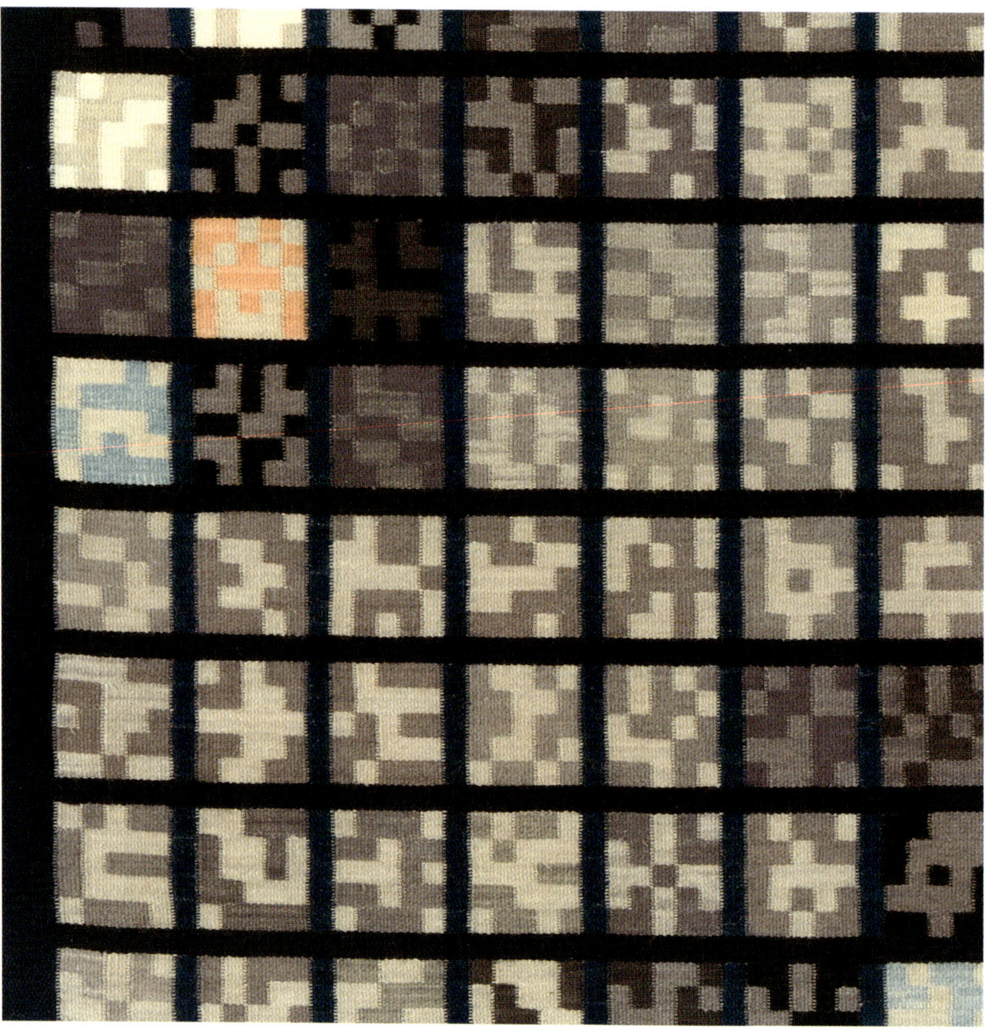

Michael F. Rohde, *Illuminative* (detail), 2020. Handwoven tapestry: 77" × 48". Cotton and wool, hand-dyed with natural dyes. Photo credit: W. Scott Miles.

KARIN SCHALLER

DAVIDSON, NORTH CAROLINA

Illuminated letters, as found in medieval manuscripts, provided the inspiration for showcasing the individual Ogham characters.

In the spring of 1997, Karin Schaller, whose *Time Capsules* we encountered in Chapter 2's "Calendars and Diaries," exhibited part of her *Ogham Alphabet* series of weavings at North Georgia College (now the University of North Georgia) in Dahlonega. From 1994 to 1996, Karin researched and designed work based on her fascination with the Ogham alphabet. For these weavings she used a 10-shaft Summer-and-Winter technique, with additional pick-up methods for letters.

In her artist statement accompanying the exhibit, she explained the alphabet: "Illuminated letters, as found in medieval manuscripts, provided the inspiration for showcasing the individual Ogham characters on exhibit. Below each woven letter was (in signage) its Roman equivalent; followed by the name of the Ogham letter in the normalized Old Irish form; then a translation of that letter name into English and, finally, the poetic kennings associated with each letter."

Karin Schaller, *Ali mac Olloman Fili Forcanas*, one of *Sanctuary Curtains: Ogham Alphabet* series of weavings, circa 1994–1996. Woven: 57" × 21.5". Silk/rayon, cotton, and metallic threads, Summer and Winter technique with pickup in areas. Courtesy of Karin Schaller.

Karin Schaller, *Ali mac Olloman Fili Forcanas* (detail), circa 1994–1996. Woven: 57" × 21.5". Silk/rayon, cotton, and metallic threads, Summer and Winter technique with pickup in areas. Courtesy of Karin Schaller.

Karin said the existing examples of the Ogham script are found on standing stones primarily in southwestern Ireland. The stones "appear to be memorials or boundary markers, and, with some exceptions, the writing occurs along the edges of the stones." She goes on to say: "Interestingly, one of the rare non-stone items on which the letters are found is a weaving wand." The script is read bottom to top.

Karin noted that the pattern areas of the hangings that make up the borders "are abstract references to the stone walls which divide the fields in rural Ireland. I was also quite taken with the other ancient structures which dot the hillsides, especially the intriguing farmsteads called ring forts, all built from the ubiquitous rocks."

Karin Schaller, *Brigit Chill Dara* (detail), one of *Sanctuary Curtains: Ogham Alphabet* series of weavings, circa 1994–1996. Woven: 41.25" × 21.5". Silk/rayon, cotton, and metallic threads, Summer and Winter technique with pickup in areas. Courtesy of Karin Schaller.

Karin Schaller, *Brigit Chill Dara* (detail). Courtesy of Karin Schaller.

Karin Schaller, *Sceilg Mhichil Solitude* (detail), one of *Sanctuary Curtains: Ogham Alphabet* series of weavings, circa 1994–1996. Woven: 50" × 21.5". Silk/rayon, cotton, and metallic threads, Summer and Winter technique with pickup in areas. Courtesy of Karin Schaller.

Karin Schaller, *Sceilg Mhichil Solitude* (detail). Courtesy of Karin Schaller.

Weaving Drafts as Codes

Readers who are weavers will understand how weave drafting is an important planning tool one can use prior to setting up a loom. Usually, contemporary weaving drafts have a bit more information than those of earlier eras. Most commonly today, one can expect to see a grid of some sort, laid out into three or four areas. Across the top is a threading draft that shows how individual warps are to be threaded on the frames or shafts of the loom. Lined up beside that, either at the left or right side, is a section called the tie-up. That indicates which of the shafts are used together in combination. Directly underneath the grid area for the tie-up is the treadling; this denotes the order of use of the shaft combinations shown in the tie-up. These three parts can be then be interpreted into a fourth part of the draft that would lie below the threading and beside the treadling to show the interaction of the warp and weft threads when woven as directed, called a drawdown.

There are variations of this basic description, of course, including that in some references the threading is shown at the bottom and the weave pattern developed above it. Instead of a tie-up area, there might be a lift-plan that shows, step by step, which shafts to use together for the picks of weft.

To the uninitiated, the grids and markings used for recording weaving patterns might seem mysterious. Probably a code of some sort, but what for and how are they used? This is often the case when scraps of paper with lines and hash marks or numbers are

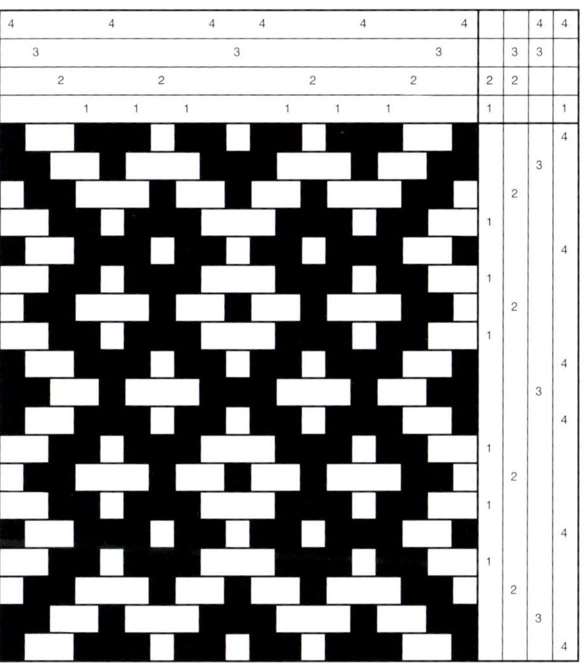

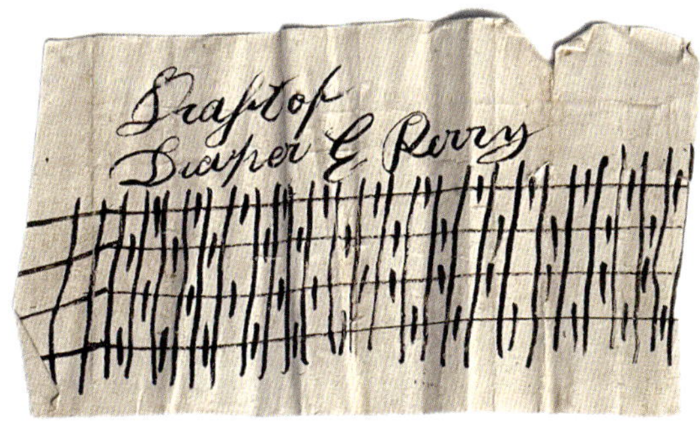

Weaving draft, ca. 1832–1893. Lorenzo Dow Davis Collection. Chestatee Regional Library, Lumpkin County Genealogy and Archives, Dahlonega, Georgia. Photo: Tommye Scanlin.

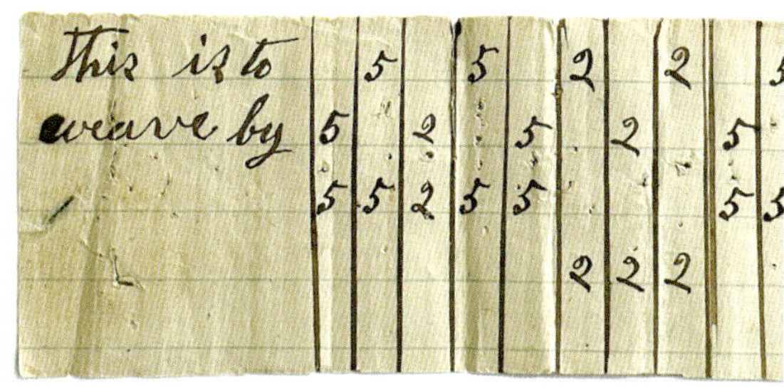

Weaving draft, ca. 1832–1893. Lorenzo Dow Davis Collection. Chestatee Regional Library, Lumpkin County Genealogy and Archives, Dahlonega, Georgia. Photo: Tommye Scanlin.

found among the records of ancestors. A few years ago this happened in our town.

A lady who was working with the archives in the public library contacted me to ask if I could look at some pieces of paper that had turned up among documents found at a flea market. She thought they were either musical notations or possibly related to weaving—especially since one of the scraps of paper had the directions "This is to weave by" written on it! They were indeed several weaving drafts, circa 1832–1893. As you can see in the ones shown here, several methods were used to indicate the way the threads would be placed on the loom. The weaver was expected to be knowledgeable enough to figure the rest of it out.

Traditional weaving patterns have been collected and passed on for many centuries. Today, there are books, magazines, and multiple online sources where one may find existing weaving drafts. However, many people like to design their own, and one way to do that is to develop a system to encode the alphabet and numerals.

As mentioned earlier, devising a code to use for planning the threading sequence is an interesting way to individualize a fabric. Code drafting or name drafting is a way to create unique designs more complex than basic plain weave (over one, under one as weft covers warp).

As an example of this, in the early 1980s members of a fiber art guild to which I belonged decided to do a "name draft" woven project. Our plan was to make friendship coverlets using woven squares with each of the participants' designed name draft. We individually designed and wove a small square using our own name draft and the colors selected by other participants, then shared those with everyone when completed.

We used overshot for the weaving technique, a traditional four-shaft weaving method that we were all familiar with. Software to assist in making the

North Georgia College Name Draft Weaving, 1986. Overshot weaving: 13" × 12". Cotton and wool. Designed and woven by Tommye Scanlin. Photo: Chris Dant.

2020

Tommye Scanlin, *Tapestry Diary-Hope is the Thing with Feathers*, 2020. Handwoven tapestry: 61.5" × 14.5" × 2" (framed). Wool and cotton. Natural dyes. Photo: Chris Dant.

weave pattern drawdowns wasn't as widely available then as now, but the art department where I was a faculty member had a computer with weaving-draft software. With my assistance, each participant entered their name codes into the drafting program so they could see the pattern results quickly and then use those to thread their looms.

As some things turn out, even though we all finished and shared our woven squares, only two of us actually put hers together! I was not one of those two—mine still live in a storage bin in my studio, these many years later.

The guild project took several months to complete and was the topic of much conversation at each of our monthly guild meetings in the meantime. Later, I used the same idea to create a draft with the name North Georgia College that students at the school wove as fundraisers for art scholarships.

Name Draft Weavings, early 1980s. Overshot weaving: 13" × 13". Cotton and wool. Yonah Mountain Fiber Art Guild members contributed weavings of their own name draft in Tommye's chosen color. Photo: Chris Dant.

5

PRACTICE: MY TAPESTRY DIARY JOURNEY

CHAPTER 5

> The ground grew thickety with minutes
> we knew no way to spend except in
> being there. A novelty of time
> kept us amused.
>
> —DANA WILDSMITH, "GPS"

I like the fact that the word "practice" is defined as both a verb and a noun. After all, when we engage in a creative practice, we are actively involved in a process that uses our hands and our senses. We make something tangible. Take a fresh look at the meaning of *practice*:

practice

/ˈpraktəs/

Transitive Verb

1a: to carry out, apply

b: to do or perform often, customarily, or habitually

2a: to perform or work at repeatedly so as to become proficient

Noun

1a: actual performance or application

b: a repeated or customary action

c: the usual way of doing something[42]

Commitment to a "repeated action" can become our "usual way of doing something."

Weaving a little bit every day for my tapestry diaries has become a usual way of doing something in my life. It is a routine I look forward to for the few minutes I devote to it daily. As I am writing this, although it is hard for me to believe, I am in the 15th year of my tapestry diary journey. Let me take you along as I describe some parts of this adventure in the next pages.

When I set up a frame loom on the first day of May in 2008 to start an experiment with a daily weaving, little did I know that I was embarking on something that would become a mainstay of my creative life. I realized what I proposed to myself was not unique. After all, many artists maintain a daily practice in their chosen medium of drawing, painting, or photography. At the time, I did not know of fabric and fiber mediums being used similarly. It was years before I heard that Kay Lawrence, an Australian artist, had woven a daily tapestry for a year—over two decades before I began my venture—or that Geri Forkner had been doing daily weavings since 2005. They describe their work earlier in the book.

In my case, for some time I had an idea to work on a tapestry in which each day would be represented by a small bit of weaving. In 2008 I decided to stop thinking about it and try it. "I'll do it for a month to satisfy my curiosity," I thought. In preparation, I put a 4-inch-wide warp on a frame loom with enough length to weave at least 31 inches. That would give me about 1 inch of weaving space to devote to each day of May, the month I chose to start.

Because of other commitments of tapestries to complete and teaching responsibilities, I did not want to have too many decisions to make as I embarked on this little weaving experiment. My solution was

Tommye Scanlin, *May* (detail of first six days), 2008. Handwoven tapestry: wool and cotton. Photo: Chris Dant.

Tommye Scanlin, *May*, 2008. Handwoven tapestry: wool and cotton. This is the first tapestry diary, done during the month of May in 2008. Photo: Chris Dant.

to make a few "rules" to follow. The first determination was to use only remnants of wefts left over from finished tapestries. I also chose to separate the days by weaving a thin black line after each day's part. The days would be represented in some "weaverly" way, such as with small shapes, thin lines, or an effect called "pick and pick" that can give an alternating pattern with each insertion of weft.

The loom was portable enough to take when I was away from home during the month so I wouldn't miss a day of weaving. What a sense of accomplishment I felt as I packed in the last few rows of weft on May 31, 2008![43] Weaving a small part every day for the month using my self-imposed rules had been an engaging activity. I was pleased with the small tapestry that resulted. Now I wondered if I would have the discipline to carry out the same idea for a year. With Yoda's quote in mind, I set about to find out: "Do. Or do not. There is no Try."

January 1st of 2009 was the starting point for the yearlong adventure. In preparation, I set up a larger loom at my home studio to accommodate a wider width and longer length for the tapestry. My plan was to weave 10 days across each row using small squares and rectangles of different widths and heights. I decided to continue to use weft remnants, as I had done for the monthlong tapestry. Each day's small bit of weaving would end with a thin horizontal line of weft, with a color change for the line each month. As I had done in the first piece from 2008, I wove either small bands or dots of color to indicate dates throughout the months.

As it turned out, within a week I realized there would be times when I could not do the weaving—either because I was out of town or simply too busy to get to the loom. Rather than give up the experiment almost before it began, I solved that dilemma by weaving a "blank" day or days with white weft in spaces equivalent to the number of missed days. Then I would continue with the current day. By the end of the year, there were many little white shapes scattered throughout the tapestry, surrounded by colorful squares and rectangles for the days I was home. All those white shapes are graphic reminders of the times I had been away and missed the daily weaving practice.

Tommye Scanlin, *Tapestry Diary*, 2009. Handwoven tapestry: 43" × 12". Wool and linen. Photo: Trevor Morris.

At the end of the year, the date and my initials were added into the tapestry by coding them with the woven dot equivalent of Braille. I also added the numerals 2009 at the top. When the tapestry was finished on December 31, 2009, I was amazed at the visual impact of the 365 small squares and rectangles. Without predesigning the image, the tapestry had become a unified composition. The patterns of thin lines and dots I had woven as the code of dates seemed like little windows in a bright, colorful city of many buildings. Although a cityscape was not the intended idea, I liked the thought.[44]

Even before the first yearlong venture ended, I knew I would continue for 2010. In the new year I still wanted to weave a little part for each day but did not want to simply repeat what was done in 2009. One modification was to make seven squares across the width, representing the seven days of the week. My plan was to continue to select yarns from remnants of past wefts, using primary and secondary hues of red, yellow, blue, orange, green, and violet in various tints and shades.

In 2010 I had several trips planned, the longest being a six-week tapestry course at West Dean College in England. For the missing days I did not want to repeat the white "blanks" done for 2009. Instead, I chose to leave empty warps for the times I was away. This gave me a technical challenge because a tapestry builds on itself as the wefts are woven. How would I be able to weave above empty warps if there were no woven support wefts underneath?

I solved the problem by weaving in thin strips of card stock for an equivalent height of the days missed once I returned home from a trip. Half hitches below and above the strips secured the spacing. The card stock strips gave the support necessary to continue the weaving above. At year's end I pulled the strips out to leave the empty warps between solidly woven day sections.

Fifty-two rows, the equivalent of 52 weeks, each row nearly 2 inches high, made the tapestry almost 90 inches long. This was over twice the length of my

Tommye Scanlin, *Tapestry Diary*, 2010. Handwoven tapestry: 89" × 11.75". Wool and linen. Photo: Trevor Morris.

2009 tapestry diary. The empty warps between the solidly woven parts were dramatic reminders of the days I had been away from home in 2010.[45]

In 2011, my plan for the year was to do individual months on a smaller frame loom so I could take the daily project with me when I traveled. I made a new warp for each month, slightly different in size but continuing the daily weaving focus. I also changed the theme for the months in a few ways. For instance, in January and February I used soumak (a technique similar to stitching on the surface but done while the tapestry is being woven) within each day's section. The January tapestry was long and narrow. The one for February differed by being shorter and wider.

As will happen when life moves on, I had an accident late in February that injured my right hand. Although my hand was bandaged for several weeks, I was still able to use my fingertips. That way I kept the daily weaving going even though the resulting tapestry for March was smaller than the others of 2011.

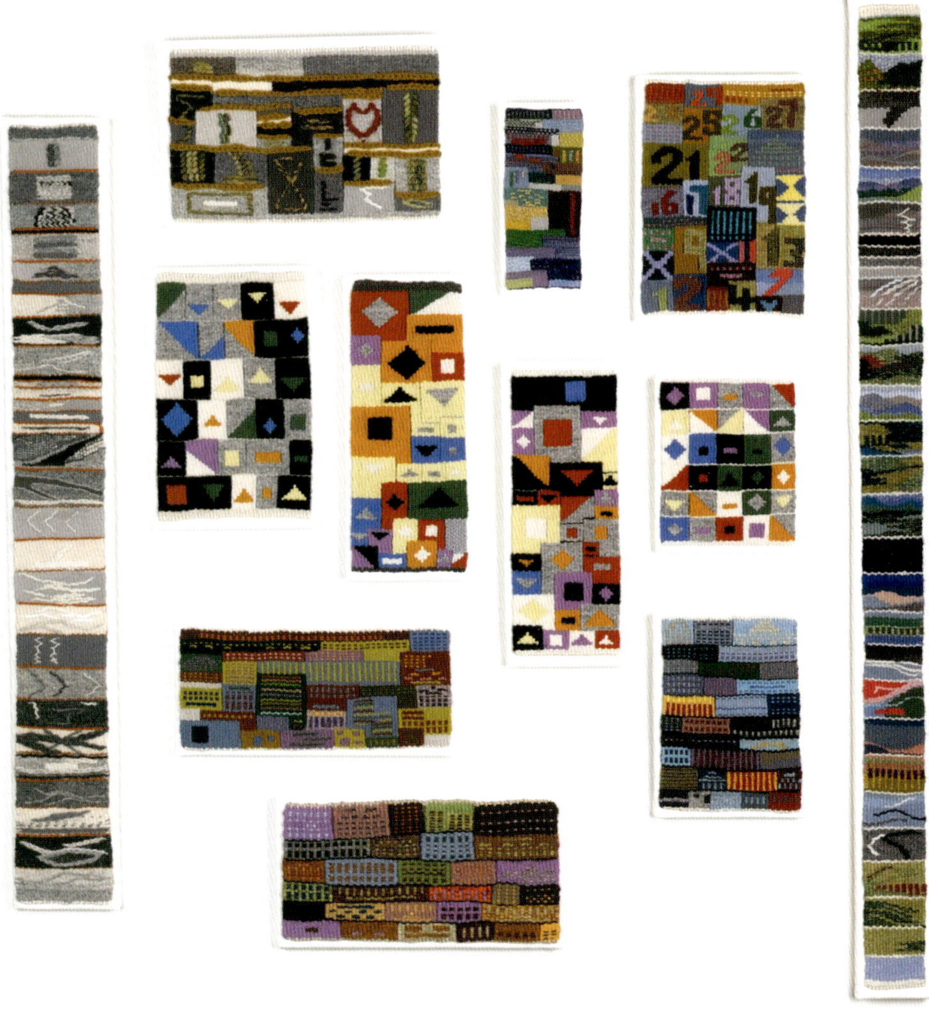

Tommye Scanlin, *Tapestry Diaries*, 2011. Handwoven tapestries: assorted sizes. Wool and cotton. During 2011 I wove individual diaries for each month. Photo: Chris Dant.

Tommye Scanlin, *May*, 2011. Handwoven tapestry: 8.25" × 6". Wool and cotton. During the month of May I used different indicators of numerals for days. Photo: Chris Dant.

For the May diary, most of the dates of the month were done with either Arabic or Roman numerals.

Tommye Scanlin, *June*, 2011. Handwoven tapestry: 9" × 6". Wool and cotton. For the months of June, July, August, and September, I cast a die to determine what to weave each day. Photo: Chris Dant.

Tommye Scanlin, *September*, 2011. Handwoven tapestry: 7" × 6". Wool and cotton. Photo: Chris Dant.

In June, July, August, and September, a tapestry in which Archie Brennan used a deck of playing cards to determine the shapes and colors to weave inspired my approach.[46] Rather than also using playing cards as prompts, I decided to assign colors and shapes to the different pips of a die. The simple shape and the color it would be woven, as well as the background color, were determined by tossing a die three times each day. My shape choices were square, rectangle, triangle, inverted triangle, diamond, or a diagonal across. Primary and secondary hues provided six color choices, each matched to a die pip. I selected red for a roll turning up a single pip, 2 gave me yellow, 3 was for blue, 4 meant I would use orange, 5 gave me green, and if 6 was rolled, I wove violet. Three neutrals—black, gray, and white—were used, and those were selected by one of two pips: 1 or 4 represented black, 2 or 5 were for gray, and I wove white if 3 or 6 turned up.

That basic plan was varied for each of those four months. In June, the first die toss indicated the shape to use; the next toss decided the color to weave the shape; the last toss indicated which neutral color to use for background. For July, the die indicated the shape to use, then which neutral color for the shape, and last, a primary/secondary color for the background. In August, alternating the shape as either a primary/secondary or neutral color and shifting the background color to the opposite made for another variation. The days were also woven in different widths and heights. Finally, for September I used the same color plan as the previous month but wove each day's part the same size.

For the remaining three months of 2011, I used pick and pick and simple stripes of color to indicate dates within a small daily background.

Tommye Scanlin, *December*, 2011. Handwoven tapestry: 4" × 8". Wool and cotton. Photo: Chris Dant.

At the end of the year, I had 12 small tapestry diaries. After seeing the result, I realized that I would rather have an entire year contained in a single tapestry. Having a length of warp filled with the 365 individual days related more closely to the passage of time I was hoping to represent. And so for the upcoming year, 2012, once again I set up the larger loom with a 12-inch-wide warp to be used continuously from month to month.

For 2012 I decided to weave a simple pictogram daily as a reminder of something from the day.[47] Although the approach took more time than the earlier, simpler small sections, now when I look back at the tapestry I can "read" what was happening throughout the year. For instance, there is the day of a dental appointment when I wove a smiling mouth. Among the woven days I can find the one when we bought a new car because it is marked with a woven green *$*. A small yellow shape was included to represent the squash found at the farmers' market one Saturday. My sister's flights to and from Alaska for vacation are shown with simplified airplane shapes woven on those days.

In addition to the pictographs, I added the date of each day by using soumak technique. This technique is done by wrapping a supplemental yarn around a selected warp in any direction, as the weaving progresses, and is a simple way to add the numbers.

To represent days away from home, I wove the number of missed days followed by an *X* upon return. For instance, I was gone for 18 days in a row during August, and those were recorded as *18 X*. In many ways, the weaving became a true diary as a visual record of the events of my life in 2012. At the end of the year, I tied a new warp length onto the old threads and in that way symbolically linked one year to the next. I've continued that practice of tying new to old warps in the years since.

In 2013, for the weft I used dye samples of wool yarn saved from years before. There were only a few yards of each color, but it was finally time to put those hundred or so colors to use. Throughout the year I changed the method of weaving the days of the month, beginning with different solid colors for each day of January. In February, I wove pick and pick to make vertical stripes with a different color combination daily. For March, I returned to solid colors. In April, I used a thin horizontal line somewhere within the larger shape for the day.

Alternating solid colors one month with another design effect for the next month gave variety to the

Tommye Scanlin, *Tapestry Diary*, 2012. Handwoven tapestry: 90" × 11". Wool, cotton, linen, metallic. The individual days are numbered using soumak technique. Pictograms representing something from the day are used in most of the daily parts. Photo: Tim Barnwell.

Tommye Scanlin, *Tapestry Diary*, 2013. Handwoven tapestry: 102" × 11.5". Wool and linen. Photo: Tim Barnwell.

tapestry. Most of the colors were repeated somewhere throughout the weaving during the year, giving visual unity to the finished piece. Linen weft was woven to represent days when I was away, and colors were again used when I returned. The neutral color and firm texture of the linen offered a nice contrast to the vibrant hues of the softer dyed wool.[48] Each day's woven section was the same size across the 12-inch width of the warp, and the 101-inch-long finished tapestry is, so far, the largest of my tapestry diaries.

In 2014 I used simple shapes, like squares, diagonals at different angles, triangles, or horizontal bands, dots, or vertical stripes each day.[49] I varied the approach each month (one month might be made up of triangles, another of pick-and-pick stripes). The wefts were once again the dye samples, except for out-of-town days, where I used alternating black and white yarns to indicate the missed days.

As I began the sixth year of tapestry diaries on January 1, 2015, I wanted a new direction. A few days into the new year's weaving, it dawned on me that design ideas from my other tapestries could be used in the daily weavings. Most of my other tapestries are inspired by the natural world, so why not use my sketches and photographs of nature forms as part of the 2015 tapestry diary?

With that in mind, I decided to do four sections for each month in which versions of a seasonal nature-related subject would be represented. For instance, four small watercolor paintings of dried oak leaves became the cartoons for January. Small squares or rectangles such as I had used with the past tapestry diaries were woven each day and surrounded the larger images as the year progressed.

Every month brought the challenge of finding an image to show in four different versions. I spent more time at the loom with this tapestry diary than with the previous ones because the larger images were slower to weave. At the end of the year, the extra time devoted to the tapestry was worth it. The overall effect of combining larger imagery with the daily blocks of color was pleasing, and I wanted to use a similar concept for the upcoming year.[50]

Tommye Scanlin, *Tapestry Diary*, 2014. Handwoven tapestry: 40.5" × 11". Wool and cotton. Photo: Tim Barnwell.

It had been demanding to weave four larger parts every month, so for 2016 I decided to simplify the idea to only one image each month, surrounded by the daily woven parts. Representing seasonal changes during the year continued to be my focus, with different aspects of the black walnut tree in our yard as the subject.

The tree is dramatic at all times of the year, from its twisted, bare limbs in winter to the clusters of brilliant yellow-green catkins of spring. The deep-green compound leaves of summer turn into a lovely golden yellow in the fall. The nuts are held in bright-green hulls as they mature, becoming dark brown and rough textured after falling and lying in the yard for a while. When the nut is cracked open, the intricacies of the interior are revealed. Many shades of brown and tan dyes can be made from the black walnut hulls; in fact, I dyed some of the weft yarns for the tapestry from hulls collected in the yard.

The yearlong observation of the black walnut tree caused me to see things about it that I had never noticed before. For instance, as the nuts form in the spring they are tiny and clustered together. The bark is deeply furrowed and dark or light gray, depending on the amount of moisture in the air. By the end of the year, I felt a deep connection to the tapestry diary because it contained many revelations about the large old tree I see every day from my kitchen window.[51]

The next year, 2017, was planned to be a busy one because several weeks at a time were on my schedule for teaching and retreats. Even so, I wanted to make a 12-inch-wide weaving on one long warp for the year, and for that I used a portable pipe loom that could be taken on my travels. I also wanted to continue the idea of day-by-day smaller parts surrounding larger images for the months.

I decided to use flowers of the season for each month, designing as the year went along wherever I happened to be at the time. Camellias bloom at home early in the year, giving me the design for January. Jonquils begin to emerge in North Georgia in February, and one became the subject for the month. When I

Tommye Scanlin, *Tapestry Diary*, on December 31, 2015, just cut off the loom. Photo: Thomas E. Scanlin.

Tommye Scanlin, *Tapestry Diary*, 2015. Handwoven tapestry: 64" × 13.5" × 2" (framed). Wool and cotton. Photo: Tim Barnwell.

was at Penland School of Crafts teaching at Spring Concentration session I found a periwinkle for the March image and grape hyacinth for April. Trillium was blooming in May and day lilies in June when I was home again. On and on throughout the year, the flowers came and went as I chose different ones for the monthly sections of the 2017 tapestry diary.

For the individual days of 2017, I recorded the weather conditions or sky color, making many variations of blue and gray throughout the tapestry. By the end of the year, the pipe loom and the tapestry diary had gone to Penland for a couple of months and to Lillian Smith Center and Hambidge Center for several weeks of artist residencies. At the end of 2017, the tapestry diary was 12 inches wide by 72 inches long and held a woven celebration of colorful flowering things I had seen throughout the year.[52]

As 2018 began, once again I set up the large loom at home for the daily tapestry. The political climate in the US had been tense for the couple of years since the previous presidential election, and it seemed that no matter which side of the political spectrum one was on, we were all throwing verbal sticks and stones at each other. To represent the discord, I chose to weave a stick or a stone each month.[53]

In the previous year, I had done quite a bit of natural dyeing and decided to use those yarns for the tapestry diary of 2018, arbitrarily selecting colors for the daily sections surrounding the monthly parts. For days when I happened to be away, I wove small sections of alternating black and white to signify the missed days.

In 2019, my inspiration for the monthly subjects was again selected from seasonally appearing flowers. However, I wanted the diary to be different from the flower-filled weaving of 2017, so for a change I photographed the subjects where they grew and included a simplified background based on the colors around each flower in situ. Natural-dyed weft yarns were again chosen both for the larger monthly images and the smaller day-by-day areas. This time, instead of

Tommye Scanlin, *Tapestry Diary*, 2016. Handwoven tapestry: 52" × 14" × 2" (framed). Wool and cotton. Photo: Tim Barnwell.

Tommye Scanlin, *Tapestry Diary*, 2017. Handwoven tapestry: 72" × 11.5". Wool, cotton, linen, metallic. Photo: Tim Barnwell.

casually choosing the colors for each individual day, I began to toss a die as I had done for the four small tapestries in 2011 to select from primary or secondary colors. I had several variations in intensity and value for each color, and after the die toss I decided which particular version of the color to use.

If you look closely and count the larger flower images for the months in 2019, you will notice there are only 11. That is because in July 2019, our much-loved cat Raymond died, a big loss for us, as he had been a part of our family for almost 18 years. I wove a black square to represent his passing but did no flower for the month.[54]

The year 2020 began innocently enough, but within a couple of months the world faced a frightful health emergency as the COVID-19 pandemic began to sweep the globe. In January I had determined to use feathers as the monthly designs for the year because I enjoy finding, photographing, and sketching feathers. Thinking about feathers always reminded me of a stanza of an Emily Dickinson poem.[55] By March 2020, as devastating effects of the virus became evident, the words of her poem were even more meaningful as I thought about the importance of being hopeful in the face of the crisis.

> 'Hope' is the thing with feathers -
>
> That perches in the soul -
>
> And sings the tune without the words -
>
> And never stops - at all -

In the larger monthly sections, except for a turkey feather that was shown smaller than life-size, each feather was woven to scale. I continued to use natural dyes chosen with a die toss and weaving a small square of alternating dark and light value of black walnut–dyed yarn on days when I was away.

The 2020 tapestry diary became one of my favorites, both because I love feathers and because it reminds me to have hope, even when things look bleakest.[56]

In 2021, I used leaves each month as the theme. For the designs I made a small painting or took a photograph of the chosen leaf at the start of each month. Events again showed up in my tapestry diary when I chronicled an emergency surgery I had in mid-August. The days of hospital stay, and later recovery time, made it impossible to weave for almost two weeks. In fact, I was not up to designing and weaving a leaf image for September. Once I was able, I wove 18 alternating gray and white squares across the width of the tapestry to represent the missing days.[57]

Tommye Scanlin, *Tapestry Diary-Sticks and Stones* (detail), 2018. Photo: Tim Barnwell.

Right: Tommye Scanlin, *Tapestry Diary-Sticks and Stones*, 2018. Handwoven tapestry: 61" × 10.75". Wool and cotton. Natural dyes. Photo: Tim Barnwell.

Far right: Tommye Scanlin, *Tapestry Diary-A Year of Flowers*, 2019. Handwoven tapestry: 60" × 11.75". Wool and cotton. Natural dyes. Photo: Tim Barnwell.

Tommye Scanlin cutting off the 2020 tapestry diary on December 31, 2020. Photo: Thomas E. Scanlin

Tommye Scanlin, *Tapestry Diary-Hope is the Thing with Feathers*, 2020. Handwoven tapestry: 61.5" × 14.5" × 2" (framed). Wool and cotton. Natural dyes. Photo: Tim Barnwell.

Tommye Scanlin, *Tapestry Diary—A Year of Leaves*, 2021. Handwoven tapestry: 59" × 11.25". Wool and cotton. Natural dyes. Photo: Tim Barnwell.

Tommye Scanlin, *Tapestry Diary—Seeds, Nuts, Fruit*, 2022. Handwoven tapestry: 56" × 11.25". Wool and cotton. Natural dyes. Photo: Tim Barnwell.

In 2022, I explored seedpods, nuts, or fruit found each month as the images for the tapestry diary. Paintings or photographs were my guides, and I continued to use natural-dyed yarn for each day, selected by the throw of a die.

In 2023 the monthly selections were designed from twigs picked up from my neighborhood, at an artist retreat, and at Arrowmont School of Arts and Crafts at different times of the year. I love the interaction of the simple twig shapes and their shadows as seen when placed on white paper to make a photograph or sketch. The small and seemingly insignificant things found during a morning walk are meaningful when and *if* I spend time noticing them. In a way, the tapestry becomes a celebration of that noticing.

Tommye Scanlin, *Tapestry Diary—2023* (detail). The Fourth of July daily entry is shown here. Several rows above you can see the empty warps still waiting for their days to come. Wool and cotton. Natural dyes. Photo: Tommye Scanlin.

As with all diaries or journals, there is more contained within them than can be described in brief passages. Most of my tapestry diaries hold small reminders of special events or remembrances meaningful only to me, as the weaver/diarist. Birthdays of loved ones are often recorded in red as if they are "Red Letter Days." Death days of important people to our lives are shown by black squares.

Some of the daily woven areas, however, symbolize events that affect many. For instance, for several years I have marked the Fourth of July by weaving red, white, and blue, and sometimes a simplified flag. The terrorist attacks of September 11, 2001, are usually noted in some way on the anniversary of that day of the year.

Now into the 16th year of daily tapestry practice, it has become an important part of my life. The commitment to it helps keep my tapestry weaving skills honed when I cannot work on a larger piece. Since 2015, I have also given myself the additional task of creating related but different images each month. The small decisions I make each day of how large to weave a section and what color to use continues to interest me. At this point, I am not sure that I will ever stop this practice—or if I would ever want to.

After all, some habits are hard to break.

Tommye McClure Scanlin,
Tapestry Diary—2023. 51" × 11.25".
Natural-dyed wool weft, linen
warp. Photo: Chris Dant.

6

WHAT'S NEXT: GETTING STARTED

CHAPTER 6

> Art is the imagination at play in the field of time. Let yourself play.
>
> —JULIA CAMERON

At this point, maybe you are thinking you want to begin a daily practice or journal with your fiber or fabric medium. Or perhaps you're considering how you could use a code system or interpret data in some textile medium. You have lots of ideas and you are eager to start—go for it, I say! If you are not sure how to begin, the following suggestions may offer promising jumping-off points. I have used several of these methods in my tapestry diaries and in other tapestry work and found them to be helpful ways to get started. You can also use these suggestions with any fiber or fabric medium. Other approaches are given on the poster printed on the reverse side of this book's jacket; see what inspires you.

These ideas or prompts offer a few starting places. Setting up "rules" makes it easier to begin and to continue, as so many of the makers have mentioned in the book. Creating your own set of rules will ultimately be your best guide. And, remember—as several pointed out: you make the rules and you can break them!

One of my favorite strategies for my tapestry diaries is to let chance play a role. For several years I have used a toss of a die to decide the color to weave for each day. Here is a more complete explanation of the process I mentioned in Chapter 5, "Practice," and how I use it:

A single six-sided die has spots or pips on each side, allowing a single die to correspond to six colors. Most often I assign primary and secondary hues of red, yellow, blue, orange, green, and violet to each pip. I have several values and intensities of each hue. I choose the variation I want to use after tossing the die to determine the color of the day.

In my color code, one pip means red, two is for yellow, and three equals blue. Orange, green, and violet are represented by four, five, or six pips.

Neutrals of black, gray, and white could be selected by having two pips representing each. For instance, one and four to mean black. Two and five indicate gray, and three and six would tell me to use white.

Having a wider range of grays available between black and white could give other variations for the die cast. Of course, any other color choice could be assigned to the pips.

I have used this die-cast method for several years to select the color for each day's small area of weaving in my tapestry diaries. I like the six colors in variations repeating at random throughout the days of the year, creating a visual medley of shapes. I am also intrigued by how often particular numbers show up on successive days.

The probability of any number turning up with a die toss is 1 out of 6, and I always wonder why occasionally one number with its associated color turns up for several days in a row.

A toss of a die as the determining factor could also indicate shapes to use.

The six pips of a die might represent simple shapes like square, rectangle, triangle, inverted triangle, diamond, or circle.

Rolling the die several times can also be done to choose the colors for the shapes and their backgrounds. Three throws of the die will give you the shape, its color, and the background color to use.

You could expand this idea with a pair of dice to give 12 options for colors. Imagine how much variety would be possible if you have several versions of each of the colors from a 12-color wheel in yarn or fabric.

Other ways to randomize your daily selections could include:

Flip a coin. If heads turns up on the coin, maybe you will use a dark value, while tails means you select a light value.

You can also make the decision of what color to select for the day by assigning numbers to different colors of yarn or fabric you have available.

Put small slips of paper with those numbers in a box, shake it up, and draw out a number, making your own personal lottery of creative direction for the day.

The number can be returned to the box to possibly be drawn again, or you can leave it out so that it is not repeated.

You can also simply write out each color name on a slip to be drawn from the box.

Another interesting daily inspiration could be a game like Wordle.

When you use fiber or fabric for projects, you often have small amounts of yarn or pieces of fabric remaining. Make a sort of grab bag of those to use for your daily focus. These remnants might not be the same size or length. Weaving or stitching with each to its end might be a prompt for the day. A fabric remnant might be used as it is, or cut to piece together with others that are randomly selected each day.

Think back to the way Kay Lawrence, whose work you saw earlier, devised a code for the alphabet to use when choosing various gray tones as she wove the poem "Monotony." Perhaps you have a favorite poem, a phrase, or even names of loved ones you would like to represent in a coded way, selecting 26 colors as the equivalents for the letters of the alphabet. Consider how you will respond to what you selected. Will you want to incorporate imagery, or symbolically represent the idea with color or texture?

Another idea is to make a list of different emotions or states of mind and assign a color to associate with each. Select one color at random each day to respond to in your ongoing piece.

As you read earlier in Chapter 3, a number of fiber and fabric artists use data on topics such as weather conditions as a starting point, with colors assigned to a temperature range. You saw examples of that approach from Joan Sheldon and Robin Lynde. The Tempestry Project works will give you many ideas to consider, whether you choose to purchase kits from them or not. You will find the photographs of countless others on social media showing temperature scarves or blankets being crocheted, knitted, or woven.[58] Photographs of temperature quilts are also widely shared; just take a look at #temperaturequilts on Instagram to find several thousand!

These are only a few suggestions. After all, it may be less threatening at the beginning if you have a plan to follow, even if vague. When you predetermine a few things to serve as your guide and give up trying to control it all, you may find that you are ready, willing, and able to start.

The point is to begin. Do something. I hope you will. I truly believe you will be enriched in many ways by beginning and maintaining a daily practice in whatever creative medium you choose.

7

AND IN THE END

CHAPTER 7

> There's a fundamental difference between the things you do every day, every single day, and the things you do only when the spirit moves you.
>
> One difference is that once you've committed to doing something daily, you find that the spirit moves you, daily. Rather than having a daily debate about today's agenda, you can decide once that you will do something, and then decide every single day *how* to do it.
>
> —SETH GODIN[59]

In the end it is often the process of doing, and not the product, that holds the most value. When you think about weaving, stitching, or piecing fabrics together, you realize that each activity takes place little by little. In many ways, that is the way we live our lives. Seconds, minutes, and hours add up to days, weeks, months, and years as we age, and these make up the fabric of our lives.

All the processes we engage in when we do fiber and fabric methods have a direct relationship to time. The things that are made are more than the individual threads or small pieces of cloth. Just as seconds add up to larger units of time, so our repeated actions of weaving, stitching, or sewing fabric together create larger objects. And those things become tangible records of our time.

In the process of making we are using time, but we are also giving ourselves time—time for our skills in a medium to grow. Through the process we also explore ideas and expand concepts. New projects might arise from ideas that had humble small beginnings in this practice. If you have started a daily practice, its routine may have become ritual for some of you. But if it did not, that is okay, too. In the end, it is about the journey. You get there by going there. Practice makes better.

Tying warp ends from a completed tapestry diary for a new year's weaving. 10/3 linen set at 8 epi, approximately 3 yards long. Photo: Tommye Scanlin.

I'm cutting off a tapestry diary at the end of the year. Endings and beginnings, over and over. Photo: Thomas E. Scanlin.

ACKNOWLEDGMENTS

As I begin to write, it's late morning and I've just finished "weaving my day" in my current tapestry diary. This has now been an ongoing morning ritual for over a decade. A few years ago, with my husband's urging, I began to document my daily practice. I have several reasons for doing my ongoing tapestry diary that I've described earlier in the book, but I also wanted to discover ways other people recognize and mark their time with textiles. It has been an inspirational quest, much of it carried out through word of mouth, by Instagram searches, and occasionally happening upon articles in magazines like *Handwoven* and *Surface Design Journal*. As a result of those searches I've been able to show examples of woven, quilted, knitted, crocheted, stitched, and mixed media works by over 25 individuals, all the while realizing that there are many others doing similar things who are not included. If you use Pinterest you might want to search for a few keywords like tapestry diary, stitch journal, and temperature quilt. On Instagram you might try #dailyweaving, #quiltjournal, #tapestrydiary, #tempestryproject, #temperaturequilt, #stitchjournal, #wovenjournal.

In the Summer 2021 issue of *Tapestry Topics*, the American Tapestry Alliance newsletter, I was the theme coordinator for a series of articles about daily practice. Several of the essay writers from the issue updated them for this book. You can find their original comments as well as those of others at this link on the American Tapestry Alliance website: https://www.americantapestryalliance.org/wp-content/uploads/2023/07/47.2-TT-Summer-2021.pdf.

My deepest gratitude goes to all those who shared their words and images to the book: Janet Austin, Ayesha Barlas, Rebecca Cartwright, Kate Colwell, Clare Daněk, Jennifer Edwards, Geri Forkner, Emma Freeman, Rowan Haug, Jess Jones, Natasha Khiev, Kay Lawrence, Robin Lynde, Mary Jane Lord, Susan Martin Maffei, Judith Martin, Jennifer McGregor, Rebecca Mezoff, Kalliopi Monoyios, Heidi Parkes, Michael Rohde, Karin Schaller, Ellen Schiffman, Joan Sheldon, Asy Connelly and Emily McNeil for the Tempestry Project, Karen Turner, Val Vaganek, and Carol Ward. Thank you to Stephanie Panlasigui for use of her photographs of the Point Reyes National Seashore Tempestries, and Erika Zambello for her photographs of the Gulf Islands National Seashore Tempestries. My appreciation goes to Christine Elizabeth Humphrys for permission to use the image of Archie Brennan's tapestry *Sonnet without Words* in the book.

I was able to work on portions of this book while in an artist residency at the Lillian E. Smith Center of Piedmont University, Clayton, Georgia, and also at Wildacres Retreat in Little Switzerland, North Carolina. Having space and time for research and writing is a special treat.

Thank you to Connie Brown, quilt maker and quilt historian, who gave me advice about "facts vs. myths" when I was seeking information about possible codes found in early quilts. I'm especially grateful to Dana Wildsmith, Annette Sanooke Clapsaddle, and Carol Crawford, all of whom taught wonderful writing workshops at John C. Campbell Folk School, both in person and online. Fellow participants in those workshops gave helpful feedback with earlier versions of a couple of chapters. Anna Garland, information specialist at the Lumpkin County Library, knew just where to find the weaving drafts in the archives; I appreciate her assistance as I photographed those.

Lova Lantz, whom I met when we were both taking a class with Dana Wildsmith, gave a careful reading and made insightful edits and comments on the manuscript. Terri and Ken Bryson, who had been first readers of my book *Tapestry Design Basics and Beyond*, gave editing help on several drafts of this one. I'm grateful for permission from Madville Publishing to use Dana Wildsmith's beautiful poem "How to Sing" from her book *With Access to Tools* as epigraph. Sarah Swett's foreword deftly portrays the aim I had for writing as she adds insight into the motivation that causes us to cherish each day by making our marks in some way.

At Schiffer Craft, senior editor Sandra Korinchak once again lent a guiding hand as I made my way through this book construction and at the end gave much-needed assistance to make finishing the book possible. Additionally, many thanks go to Llara Pazdan for the beautiful design and layout to cause the whole thing to come to life.

As I wrap up the last details of the book, I must mention once more how my husband has seen me through the last couple of years of writing by boosting me along when I was discouraged, picking up pizza for us both when I stayed late at the computer, and always keeping me supplied with dark chocolate truffles. His patience and encouragement in all things, all the time, mean the world to me. Thank you, Thomas.

Opposite: Tommye Scanlin, *May* (detail), 2008. Handwoven tapestry: Wool and cotton. Photo: Chris Dant.

APPENDIX 1

MORSE CODE

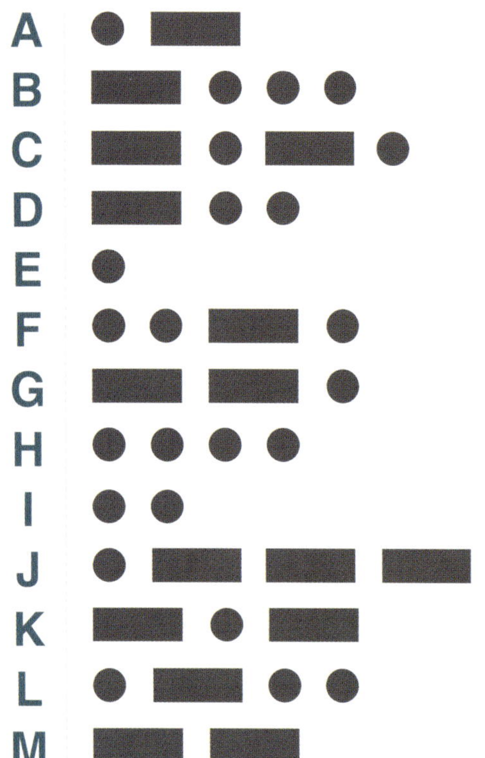

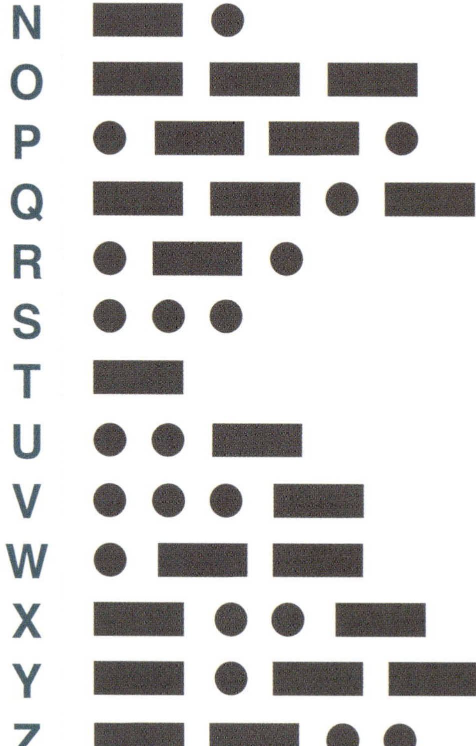

APPENDIX 2

BRAILLE ALPHABET CHART AND GRID

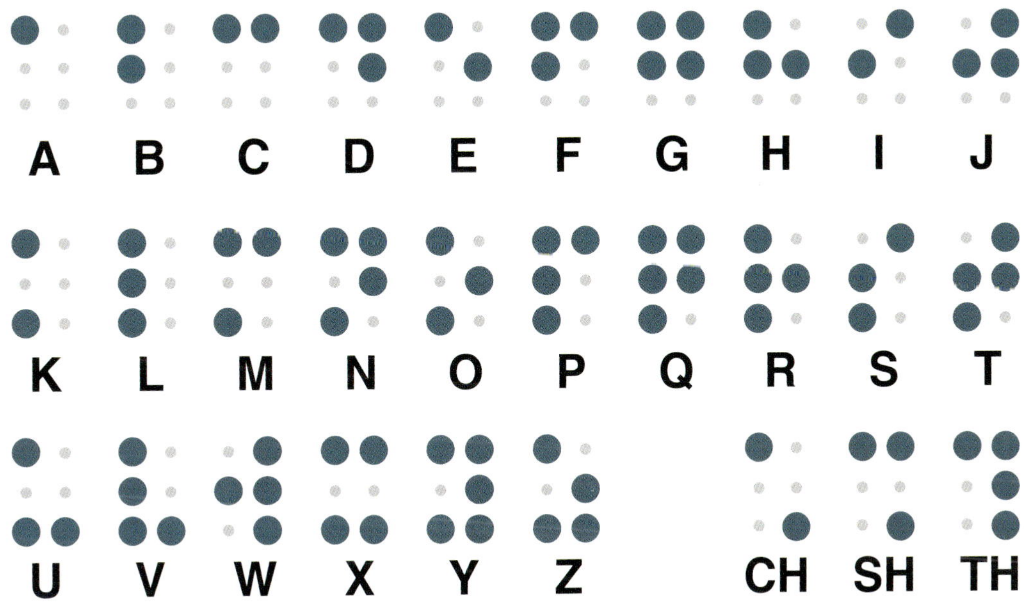

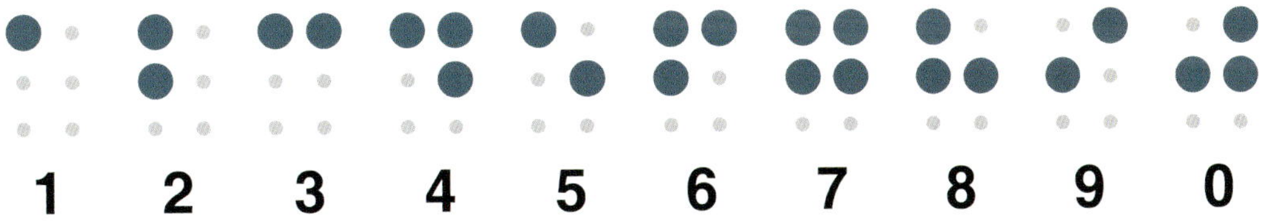

HOW TO USE THE BRAILLE ALPHABET

The braille alphabet consists of six dots, which are numbered vertically.

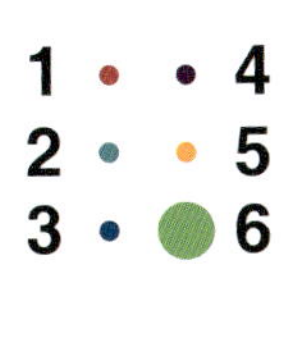

The capital letter indicator, dot 6, placed before a letter makes a capital letter.

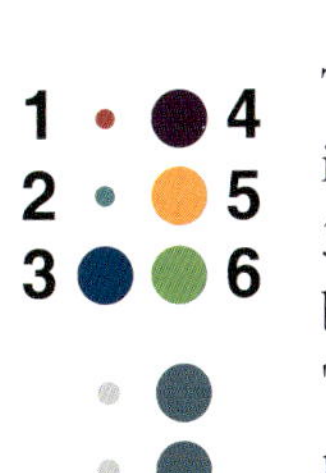

The numeric indicator, dots 3-4-5-6, placed before the characters "a" through "j" makes the numbers 1 through 0.

APPENDIX 3

USEFUL TEMPLATES

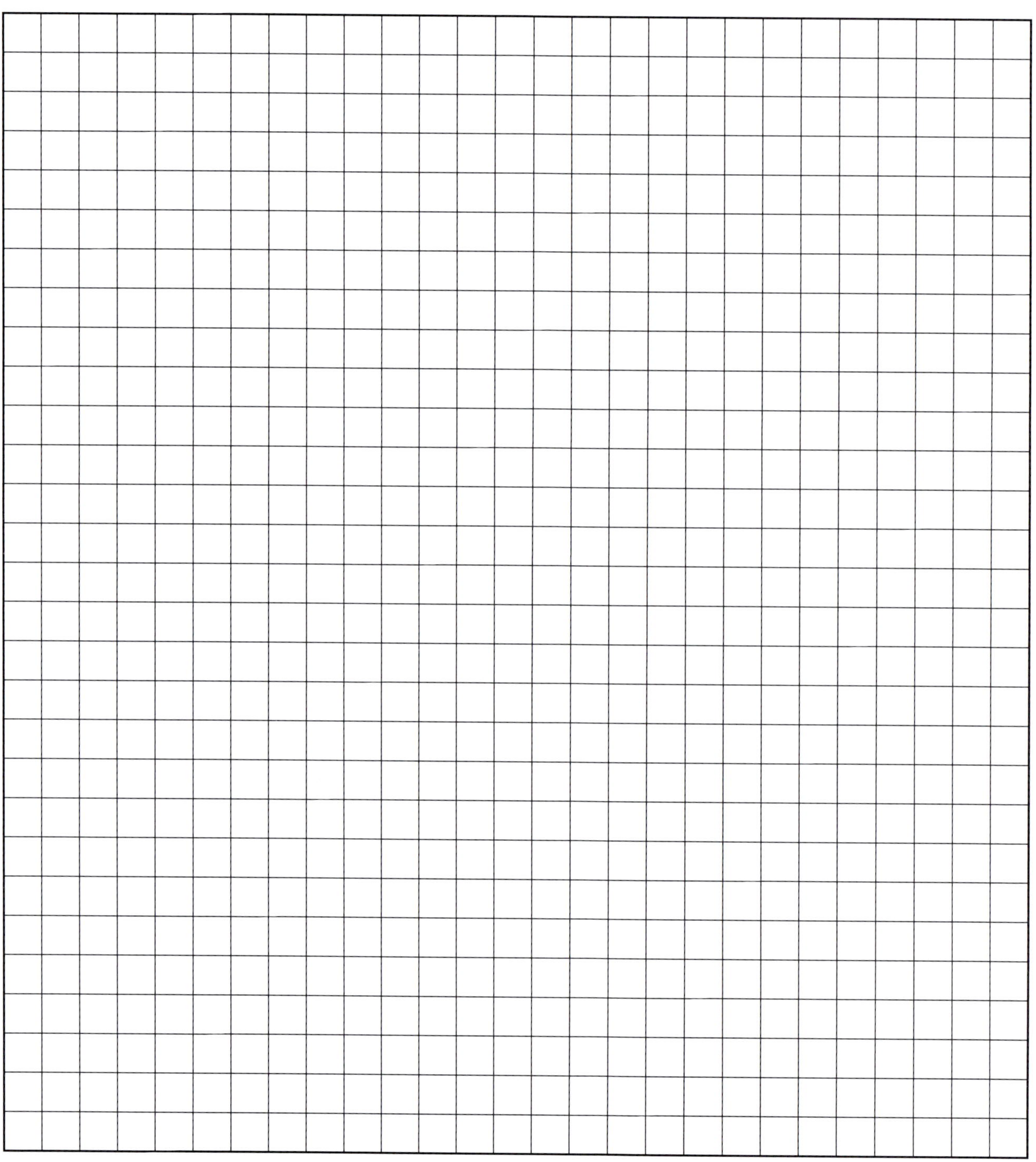

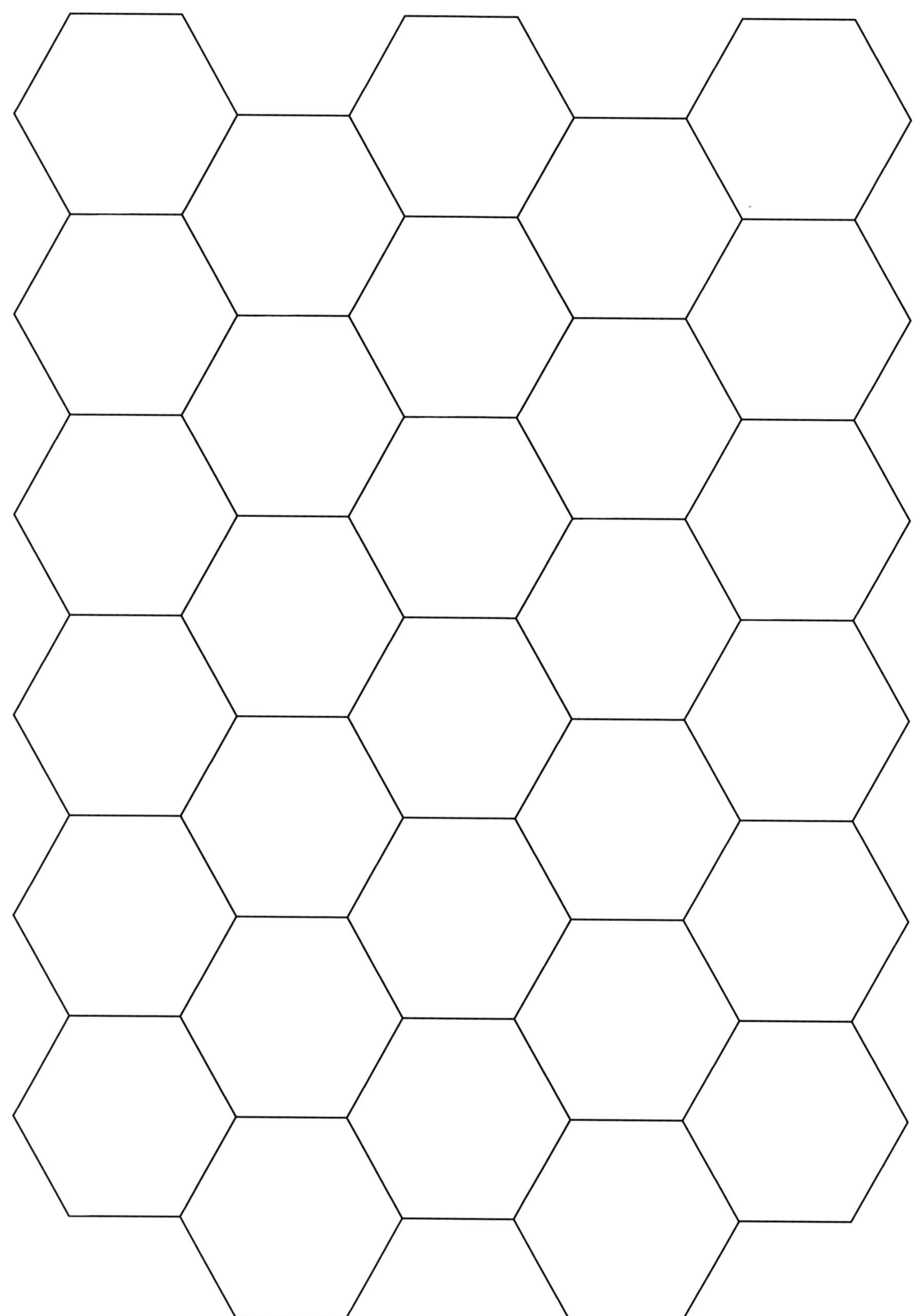

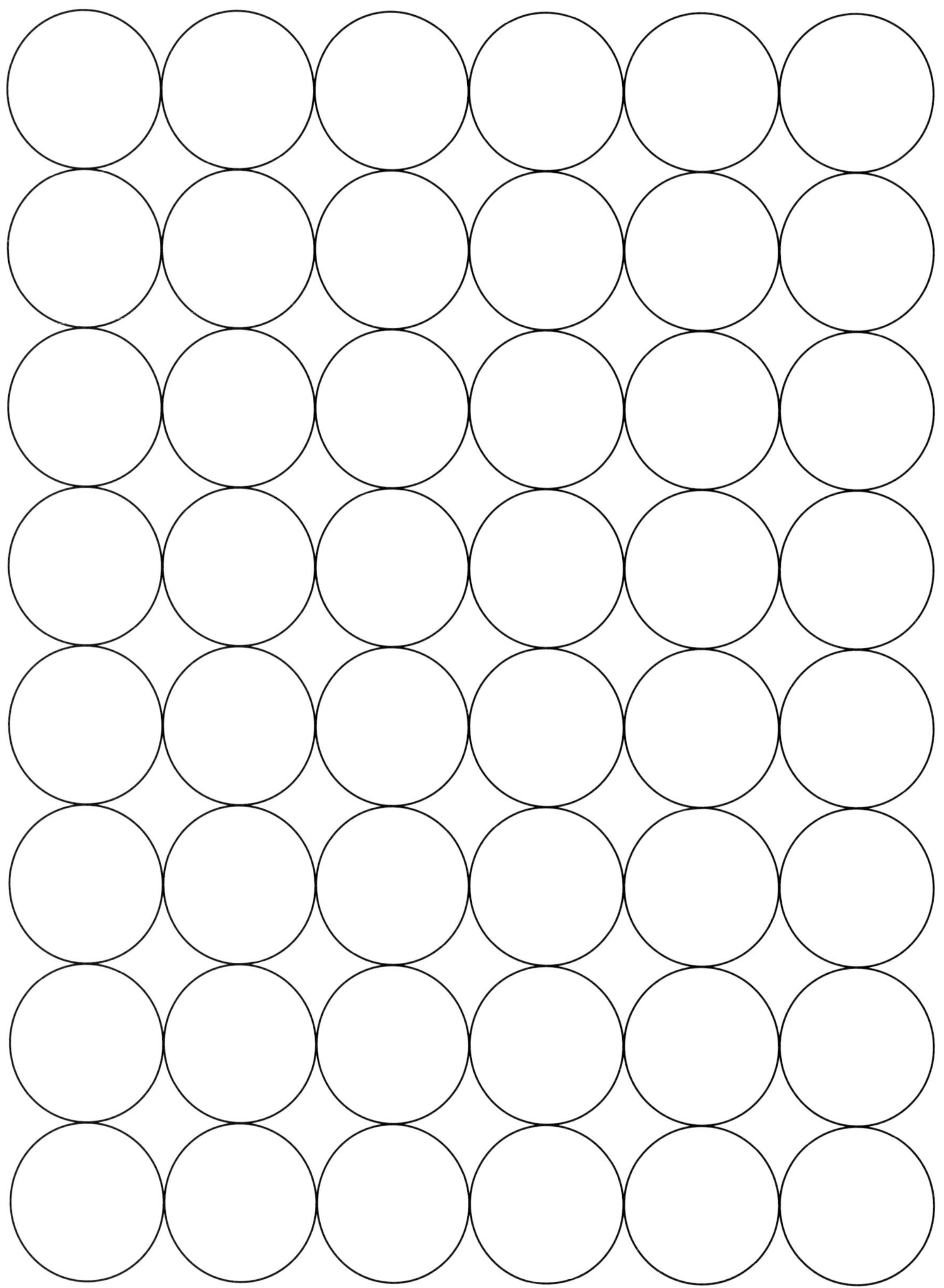

RESOURCES

There are so many things to inspire us in the print and internet world! I frequently seek out anything that will give me insight into creative process, whether for my daily practice or my other "regular" art making. This list of resources is only a starting point. The internet links were current as of this writing, but we know those can change quickly.

Inspiration and Ideas

About Time, podcast, www.timelyapp.com/podcasts.

Bayeux Tapestry, https://www.bayeuxmuseum.com/en/.

Bayles, David, and Ted Orland. *Art & Fear: Observations on the Perils (and Rewards) of Artmaking*. Image Continuum, 1993.

Beam, Mary Todd. *Celebrate Your Creative Self*. Cincinnati: North Light Books, 2001.

Cameron, Julia. *The Artist's Way*. Tarcher/Putnam Books, 1992.

Dunnewold, Jane. *Creative Strength Training: Prompts, Exercises and Personal Stories for Encouraging Artistic Genius*. Cincinnati: North Light Books, 2016.

Hillis, Nancy. *The Artist's Journey: Bold Strokes to Spark Creativity*. Artist's Journey Press, 2018.

Holmes, Cassie. *Happier Hour: How to Beat Distraction, Expand Your Time, and Focus on What Matters Most*. New York: Gallery Books, 2022.

Kretz, Kate. *Art from Your Core: A Holistic Guide to Visual Voice*. Chicago, IL: Intellect, The University of Chicago Press, 2024.

McNiff, Shaun. *Trust the Process: An Artist's Guide to Letting Go*. Boulder, CO: Shambhala, 1998.

Redmond, Lea. *Knit the Sky: Cultivate Your Creativity with a Playful Way of Knitting*. North Adams, MA: Storey, 2015.

Sidore, Micala. *The Art Is the Cloth*. Atglen, PA: Schiffer Craft, 2020.

Calendars, Diaries, Journals Information

American Tapestry Alliance. "The Tapestry Diary: It's about Time." https://americantapestryalliance.org/tapestry-education/educational-articles-on-tapestry-weaving/the-tapestry-diary-its-about-time.

"Daily Practice: What's Yours?" *Tapestry Topics*. Tommye Scanlin, theme coordinator. American Tapestry Alliance. Summer 2022. https://www.americantapestryalliance.org/wp-content/uploads/2023/07/47.2-TT-Summer-2021.pdf.

"The Daily Quilt: Heidi Parkes Explores Storytelling through Textiles and Hand Stitches." *Threads Magazine*, Spring 2023.

Daněk. Clare. "Stitching as Reflection and Resistance." In *Crafting Autoethnography: Processes and Practices of Making Self and Culture*, edited by Jackie Goode, Karen Lumsden, and Jan Bradford, 121–131. London: Routledge, 2023.

Ludwig, L. K. *True Vision: Authentic Art Journaling*. Beverly, MA: Quarry Books, 2008.

McDonald, Quinn. *Raw Art Journaling: Making Meaning, Making Art*. Cincinnati: North Light Books, 2011.

Data Visualization Information

Data.gov is the United States government's open-data website—https://data.gov.

Date and Time website—https://www.timeanddate.com/.

Farmers Almanac website—https://www.farmersalmanac.com/weather-history.

Farmers Almanac Moon Phases: https://www.farmersalmanac.com/calendar/moon-phases.

Friendly, Michael, and Howard Wainer. *A History of Data Visualization and Graphic Communication*. Cambridge, MA: Harvard University Press, 2021.

Infogram website, "18 Surprising Data Visualizations in Your Everyday Life" by Marisa Krystian —https://infogram.com/blog/18-surprising-data-visualizations-in-your-every-day-life.

Joan Sheldon Fiber Designs website, "The Globally Warm Scarf"—http://sheldonfiberdesigns.net/the-globally-warm-scarf.

NASA Goddard Institute of Space Studies Datasets and Images—https://data.giss.nasa.gov.

National Oceanic and Atmospheric Administration—https://www.ncdc.noaa.gov/cdo-web.

New Atlas website, "Art in the Age of Ones and Zeroes: Turning Big Data into Art" by Rich Haridy—https://newatlas.com/art-ones-and-zeros-data-visualization/49926.

Quilting Daily website—https://www.quiltingdaily.com/how-to-make-a-temperature-quilt.

Scientific American, "A Chronicle of Timekeeping" by William J. H. Andrewes—https://www.scientificamerican.com/article/a-chronicle-of-timekeeping-2006-02.

TED Art Made of Data presentations—https://www.ted.com/playlists/201/art_from_data.

The Tempestry Project website—https://www.tempestry-project.com/product/national-parks-tempestry-project-book.

Tufte, Edward Rolf. *The Visual Display of Quantitative Information*. Cheshire, CT: Graphics Press, 1983.

The Twiddletails Blog—https://twiddletails.blogspot.com/2019/12/temperature-quilt-how-to-obtain-weather.html.

Weather Underground—https://www.wunderground.com/history.

Wikipedia, "Climate Change Art"—https://en.wikipedia.org/wiki/Climate_change_art.

Zambello, Erika. *The National Parks Tempestry Project: A Community Climate Change Initiative*. 2022.

Code and Symbol Information

British Council, Anyone/Anywhere. "Telling Stories with Numbers: Five Artists Using Big Data"—https://www.britishcouncil.org/anyone-anywhere/explore/digital-creativity/telling-stories-numbers.

Burns, Mary F. *Burns Braille Guide: A Quick Reference to Unified English Braille*. New York: American Foundation for the Blind Press, 2015. Proust Ebook Central.

Coe, Margaret, CoeWeaves. Online Calculators, including Golden Ratio and Fibonacci. Accessed July 13, 2023. https://coeweaves.com/resources.

Cunliffe, Jordan. *Record, Map, and Capture in Textile Art: Data Visualization in Cloth and Stitch*. London: Batsford, 2022.

Digital Archives of Documents Related to Name Drafting. https://www2.cs.arizona.edu/patterns/weaving/wtopic_name.html.

Frutiger, Adrian. *Signs and Symbols: Their Design and Meaning*. Translated by Andrew Bluhm. New York: Watson-Guptill, 1998.

Knott, Ron. "Fibonacci Numbers and Nature." https://r-knott.surrey.ac.uk/Fibonacci/fibnat.html.

Liungman, Carl G. *Dictionary of Symbols*. New York: W.W. Norton, 1991.

MacLeod, Kevin. Incompetech website for graph paper and more. https://incompetech.com/graphpaper.

National Library Service for the Blind and Print Disabled, Library of Congress—https://www.loc.gov/nls/resources/blindness-and-vision-impairment/braille-information.

Robinson, Andrew. *Lost Languages: The Enigma of the World's Undeciphered Scripts*. New York: McGraw-Hill, 2002.

Shepherd, Rowena, and Rupert Shepherd. *1000 Symbols: What Shapes Mean in Art & Myth*, New York: Thames & Hudson, 2002.

Stuff. "Pippa's Astonishing Story Recognised" by Michael Field—https://www.stuff.co.nz/national/63516307/pippas-astonishing-story-recognised.

Tresidder, Jack. *Dictionary of Symbols: An Illustrated Guide to Traditional Images, Icons, and Emblems*. San Francisco: Chronicle Books, 1998.

Wikipedia, "Morse Code"—https://en.wikipedia.org/wiki/Morse_code.

Technique Resources

Bonesteel, Georgia. *Scrap Happy Quilts*. Atglen, PA: Schiffer Craft, 2018.

Brandeis, Susan. *The Intentional Thread: A Guide to Drawing, Gesture, and Color in Stitch*. Atglen, PA: Schiffer Craft, 2019.

Daly, Fiona. *Weaving on a Little Loom: Techniques, Patterns, and Projects for Beginners*. Quarto Publishing Group UK, 2018.

Mezoff, Rebecca. *The Art of Tapestry Weaving*. North Adams, MA: Storey, 2020.

Shirley, Shannon. *Celebrate the Day with Quilts: An Art Quilt Challenge*. Atglen, PA: Schiffer, 2014.

Wellesley-Smith, Claire. *Resilient Stitch: Wellbeing and Connection in Textile Art*. London: Batsford, 2021.

Wellesley-Smith, Claire. *Slow Stitch: Mindful and Contemplative Textile Art*. London: Batsford, 2015.

NOTES

1. Dana Wildsmith, *With Access to Tools: Poems* (Lake Dallas: Madville, 2023).

2. Amanda Gorman, "New Day's Lyric," 2022, https://www.cnn.com/style/article/amanda-gorman-new-days-lyric-poem-cec/index.html.

3. Duane Keiser is an artist who's become known for his small paintings done each day. https://www.duanekeiser.com/a-painting-a-day.

4. https://www.gistyarn.com/blogs/journal/daily-tapestry-weavings-an-interview-with-natasha-khiev-of-mighty-loom.

5. Opening lines of the American television soap opera *Days of Our Lives*.

6. Julia Cameron, https://www.theartistswaybook.com/.

7. http://oxforddictionaries.com/words/the-oec-facts-about-the-language.

8. https://www.scientificamerican.com/article/a-chronicle-of-timekeeping-2006-02/. Article was originally published with the title "A Chronicle of Timekeeping" in *SA Special Editions* 16, no.1s (February 2006), 46–55, doi:10.1038/scientificamerican0206-46sp.

9. https://en.wikipedia.org/wiki/Diary_of_Merer.

10. Siying Chen, Yun Su, Xiuqi Fang, and Jia He, "Climate Records in Ancient Chinese Diaries and Their Application in Historical Climate Reconstruction—a Case Study of Yunshan Diary," *Climate of the Past* 16 (2020): 1873–1887, doi: 10.5194/cp-16-1873-2020.

11. S. Pepys and R. Le Gallienne, *Passages from the Diary of Samuel Pepys* (New York: Modern Library, 1923), https://hdl.handle.net/2027/mdp.49015000236431.

12. https://www.intensivejournal.org/index.php.

13. https://www.npr.org/sections/goatsandsoda/2022/12/22/1139781319/can-dogs-smell-time-just-ask-donut-the-dog.

14. Clare Daněk, "Stitching as Reflection and Resistance: The Use of a Stitch Journal during Doctoral Study," in Jackie Goode, Karen Lumsden and Jan Bradford, eds., *Crafting Autoethnography: Process and Practices for Making Self and Culture* (London: Routledge, 2023), 121–131. Daněk describes the evolution of her stitch journal at the website http://www.claredanek.me/stitch-journal.

15. Edward R. Tufte, *The Visual Display of Quantitative Information* (Cheshire, CT: Graphics Press, 1983), 177.

16. Michael Friendly and Howard Wainer, *A History of Data Visualization and Graphic Communication* (Cambridge, MA: Harvard University Press, 2021), 11.

17. Tufte, 9.

18. www.ncdc.noaa.gov/cdo-web/search.

19. https://medium.com/@Infogram/meet-6-artists-who-have-swept-data-art-into-the-digital-age-d5c5ae805bab.

20. https://www.nathaliemiebach.com/.

21. https://www.tempestryproject.com/about/.

22. Take a look at #temperaturequilt to find many examples.

23. https://curatedquilts.com/blogs/news/it-s-getting-hot-in-here-temperature-quilts-from-quiltcon-2022.

24. M. E. Mann and P. D. Jones, "Global Surface Temperatures over the Past Two Millennia," *Geophysical Research Letters* 30, no. 15 (2023): 1820.

25. https://www.nationalparkstraveler.org/2019/07/over-100-crafters-sign-create-national-park-tempestries.

26. https://www.tempestryproject.com/product/national-parks-tempestry-project-book/.

27. Jordan Cunliffe, *Record, Map & Capture in Textile Art: Data Visualization in Cloth and Stitch* (London: Batsford, 2022), 26.

28. https://www.britannica.com/technology/Analytical-Engine.

29. https://ageofrevolution.org/200-object/jacquard-loom/.

30. https://www.britannica.com/technology/Jacquard-loom.

31. Cunliffe, *Record, Map & Capture in Textile Art*, 89.

32. https://www.britannica.com/biography/Ada-Lovelace.

33. https://www.theguardian.com/childrens-books-site/2015/sep/10/top-10-codes-keys-and-ciphers.

34. The Book of Ballymote manuscript from the 14th century is the source of most of what is known about Ogham. It explained how the Ogham letters corresponded to letters of the Latin alphabet.

35. https://en.wikipedia.org/wiki/Morse_code.

36. Incahuasi in the Cañete Valley, https://youtube/AmPyz1kCbOw.

37. Gordon A. J. Petersen and Marshall McClintock, *A Guide to Codes and Signals: International Flag Code, Secret Ciphers, Weather Signals, Morse Code, Sign Language, etc., with Flags of All Nations* (Racine, WI: Whitman, 1942), https://babel.hathitrust.org/cgi/pt?id=mdp.39015008612817&view=1up&seq=1.

38. Sally Coulthard, *A Short History of the World According to Sheep* (London: Head of Zeus, 2020), 165–166.

39. Basics for name drafting are given in appendix 3.

40. Antique weaving drafts shown are not name drafts but illustrate the various marks serving as codes to tell the weaver how to thread a loom to create a specific pattern. These are from the Lorenzo Dow Davis Collection, series 1, box 3 (1832–1893), held in the archives of the Chestatee Regional Library System, Lumpkin County Library, Dahlonega, Georgia. These were hand-drawn by Susan Davis.

41. Archie Brennan as told to Brenda Osborn, *Archie Brennan: Tapestry as Modern Art* (Atglen, PA: Schiffer, 2021), 131.

42. Merriam-Webster.com Dictionary, s.v. "Practice," accessed August 7, 2022, https://www.merriam-webster.com/dictionary/practice.

43. I wrote about this in my blog in 2008: https://tapestry13.blogspot.com/2008/05/more-about-calendarjournal-tapestry.html.

44. https://tapestry13.blogspot.com/2010/01/tapestry-diary-for-2009-off-loom-next.html.

45. https://tapestry13.blogspot.com/2011/12/tapestry-diary-year-three-is-completed.html.

46. Brenda Osborn, *Archie Brennan*.

47. https://tapestry13.blogspot.com/2012/12/one-more-year-is-history-almost.html.

48. https://tapestry13.blogspot.com/2013/12/2013-tapestry-diary-is-off-loom.html.

49. https://tapestry13.blogspot.com/2014/12/the-value-of-daily.html.

50. https://tapestry13.blogspot.com/2016/01/how-long-did-it-take-you-to-do-that.html.

51. https://tapestry13.blogspot.com/2016/12/happy-end-of-2016.html.

52. https://tapestry13.blogspot.com/2017/12/out-with-old-in-with-new.html.

53. https://tapestry13.blogspot.com/2018/12/happy-new-year-may-it-be-better-one.html.

54. https://tapestry13.blogspot.com/2020/01/and-so-it-begins-again.html.

55. Emily Dickinson, "'Hope' is the thing with feathers" in *The Complete Poems of Emily Dickinson*, ed. Thomas H. Johnson (Cambridge, MA: Belknap Press of Harvard University Press, 1951). copyright © 1951, 1955, 1979, 1983 by the President and Fellows of Harvard College, reprinted by permissions of the publishers and Trustees of Amherst College.

56. https://tapestry13.blogspot.com/2021/02/months-pass-before-you-know-it.html.

57. https://tapestry13.blogspot.com/2022/01/happy-new-year-may-it-be-better-than.html.

58. https://mymodernmet.com/temperature-blanket-knitting-crochet/.

59. https://seths.blog/2014/12/daily/.

BIBLIOGRAPHY

Andrewes, William J. H. "A Chronicle of Time Keeping." *Scientific American*, February 1, 2006. Accessed July 13, 2023. https://www.scientificamerican.com/article/a-chronicle-of-timekeeping-2006-02/.

Auther, Elissa. "Andean Weaving and the Appropriation of the Ancient Past in Modern Fiber Art." *Bauhaus Imaginista Journal*. Accessed July 13, 2023. https://www.bauhaus-imaginista.org/articles/824/andean-weaving-and-the-appropriation-of-the-ancient-past-in-modern-fiber-art.

Cameron, Julia. *The Artist's Way*. New York: Tarcher-Perigee, 2016.

Coe, Margaret. CoeWeaves Online Calculators, including Golden Ratio and Fibonacci. Accessed July 13, 2023. https://coeweaves.com/resources.

Cunliffe, Jordan. *Record, Map, and Capture in Textile Art: Data Visualization in Cloth and Stitch*. London: Batsford, 2022.

Daněk, Clare. "Stitching as Reflection and Resistance." In *Crafting Autoethnography: Processes and Practices of Making Self and Culture*, edited by Jackie Goode, Karen Lumsden, and Jan Bradford, 121–131. London: Routledge, 2023.

Digital Archives of Documents Related to Name Drafting. Accessed July 13, 2023. https://www2.cs.arizona.edu/patterns/weaving/wtopic_name.html.

Eikmeier, Barbara J. "How to Make a Temperature Quilt." *Quilting Daily*. Accessed July 13, 2023. https://www.quiltingdaily.com/how-to-make-a-temperature-quilt.

Friendly, Michael, and Howard Wainer. *A History of Data Visualization and Graphic Communication*. Cambridge, MA: Harvard University Press, 2021.

Knott, Ron. "Fibonacci Numbers and Nature." Accessed July 13, 2023. https://r-knott.surrey.ac.uk/Fibonacci/fibnat.html.

MacLeod, Kevin. Incompetech website for graph paper and more. Accessed July 13, 2023. https://incompetech.com/graphpaper/

Martin, Judy. *A Poem About Time: Not to Know but to Go On*. Printed by the author. Manitoulin Island, ON: 2018. www.judithmartin.info.

McDonald, Quinn. *Raw Art Journaling: Making Meaning, Making Art*. Cincinnati: North Light Books, 2011.

National Braille Press. Accessed July 13, 2023. https://www.nbp.org.

Parkes, Heidi. "The Daily Quilt: Heidi Parkes Explores Storytelling Through Textiles and Hand Stitches." *Threads Magazine*, Spring 2023.

Redmond, Lea. *Knit the Sky: Cultivate Your Creativity with a Playful Way of Knitting*. North Adams, MA: Storey, 2015.

Scanlin, Tommye McClure. "Designing by Chance." *Handwoven Magazine*, June 2, 2021. https://handwovenmagazine.com/designing-by-chance.

———. "Time Warp and Weft—A Celebration of the Passage of Time through Weaving." *Shuttle Spindle and Dyepot*, Summer 2017.

Scanlin, Tommye McClure, theme coordinator. "Daily Practice: What's Yours?" *Tapestry Topics*, American Tapestry Alliance, Summer 2021. Accessed July 13, 2023. https://www.americantapestryalliance.org/wp-content/uploads/2023/07/47.2-TT-Summer-2021.pdf.

Sheldon, Joan. "The Globally Warm Scarf." Sheldon Fiber Designs. Accessed July 13, 2023. http://sheldonfiberdesigns.net/the-globally-warm-scarf/.

Tempestry Project, The. Accessed July 13, 2023. https://www.tempestryproject.com/.

Tufte, Edward Rolf. *The Visual Display of Quantitative Information*. Cheshire, CT: Graphics Press, 1983.

Wikipedia. "Morse Code." Accessed July 13, 2023. https://en.wikipedia.org/wiki/Morse_code.

Wildsmith, Dana. *With Access to Tools: Poems*. Lake Dallas: Madville, 2023.

Zambello, Erika. *The National Parks Tempestry Project: A Community Climate Change Initiative*. 2022. Available from The Tempestry Project. https://www.tempestryproject.com/product/national-parks-tempestry-project-book.

INDEX TO CONTRIBUTORS' WORKS

INDEX